LOGIC PROBLEMS
FOR DRILL AND REVIEW

James Hall

UNIVERSITY
PRESS OF
AMERICA

Copyright © 1991 by
University Press of America®, Inc.
4720 Boston Way
Lanham, Maryland 20706

3 Henrietta Street
London WC2E 8LU England

Library of Congress Cataloging-in-Publication Data

Hall, James, 1933-
Logic problems for drill and review / James Hall.
p. cm.
1. Logic—Study and teaching   I. Title.
BC59.H35   1991
160'.76—dc20   91-23772 CIP

ISBN 0-8191-8379-2 (pbk., alk. paper)

INTRODUCTORY NOTES

To the Instructor:

The most regular and frequent request that I have had from my logic students over the last twenty seven years has been for extra problems on which they could practice their beginners' skills. I have used many different texts along the way; but, however generous they have been in providing exercises, I always seem to use them up for graded homework. To fill the gap, I have written a lot of problems.

Students who have done an extra dozen (or hundred) exercises want to know whether their solutions are proper. Initially, I was willing to go over their extra work with them, to give them the reinforcement that they both wanted and deserved. As a result, they improved their work (and their rewards); and, as a result of that, everybody wanted on board. So, eventually, I found myself with more papers to check than domestic tranquility could tolerate. So problem sets became problem-and-solution sets—not as effective as one-on-one conferences, but more feasible in a harried schedule.

This book consists of 220 such problems, with at least one solution each. I believe that using it will help your students and save your time. I hope that you (and they) will send suggestions. I have a few hundred more problems simmering; and I would love to enrich and vary the stock.

I am indebted to the Universities of Richmond and Warwick, respectively, for the time and a place to put this collection together. I have further debts: to Irving Copi (obvious), to my students (visible from time to time), and to my colleagues (they know who). I dedicate this book to them all, and to all those others who take delight in puzzles.

To the Student:

The point of this book is to provide you with extra arguments for exercise and review. It is a supplementary resource, not a text, that should be especially useful for practice before tests and examinations. Most students find immediate reinforcement encouraging and instructive; so I have provided at least one solution for each problem. But one cannot learn to construct proofs simply by looking at ones that have already been worked out. Consequently, the solutions are relegated to the back of the book. Those who peek before doing their own work will defeat the purpose of the enterprise.

The problems will yield to the treatments found in any text; but logic problems have multiple solutions. There is more than one way around most barns. Instructors who are using certain texts may bar some operations that I allow in proof construction. When that is the case, a legal proof will often differ from the one shown here—usually by having added steps of Commutation and Double Negation. My own way of constructing proofs depends on many presuppositions which, however orthodox, ought to be made explicit. The first chapter provides for that, along with a review of all the rules and how they work.

Then it will be time to get on with the problems. The earliest ones are very easy; but they get progressively harder. Toward the end, especially if you forswear all forms of conditional proof, they are very hard indeed. But your skills will be improving, too. (Lots of) practice still makes perfect.

Kenilworth, Warks., 1990

TABLE OF CONTENTS

ONE: THE APPARATUS

A. Basic Laws and Truth Tables.

All the proofs rest on four basic laws (axioms, postulates, conventions):

1. The Law of Identity. In a fixed context, the truth value of a proposition cannot change. If p is true in a setting, then it is true throughout that setting; and if it is false there, then it is false throughout.

2. The Law of Excluded Middle. True and False are the only truth values recognized here, even though 'true' and 'false' are not complementary in all domains. The general complement of 'true' is 'not-true,' and the set of false utterances is only a proper subset of the not-true set. So we ignore "non-propositional" utterances (which may, or may not, have a logic of their own). Further, among propositions, only all those which are true or false count. We relegate all others (if any) to the domain of more complex logics.

3. The Law of Contradiction. The negation of any true proposition is false, and the negation of any false one is true.

4. The Law of Transitive Equivalence. Any two things that are equivalent to a third thing are equivalent to each other.

The first three of these laws are the ground rules for constructing truth tables. The law of identity says a proposition must have the same truth value throughout any one row of any truth table. The law of excluded middle says **T** and **F** are the only values allowed in a table. The law of contradiction determines the table value of the negation of any proposition whose own table value is already settled. Truth tables themselves have two basic uses: to define the logical operators that are used in proof symbolization, and to justify the basic rules for substitution and inference that are used in proof construction.

B. Definitions of the Logical Operators.

Using 'p', 'q' and 'r' as propositional variables, '~' and '·' are defined directly. The remaining operators ('∨', '⊃' and '≡') are short-hand expressions of longer strings which employ only '~' and '·'. Their redundancy is usually ignored because using them makes proofs shorter (and encourages symbolizations that closely follow the natural flow of what is being symbolized).

~

p	~p
T	F
F	T

·

p	q	p · q
T	T	T
T	F	F
F	T	F
F	F	F

∨

p	q	p ∨ q	or	~(~p	·	~q)
T	T	T		T		F
T	F	T		T		F
F	T	T		T		F
F	F	F		F		T

⊃

p	q	p ⊃ q	or	~(p	·	~q)
T	T	T		T		F
T	F	F		F		T
F	T	T		T		F
F	F	T		T		F

≡

p	q	p ≡ q	or	~(p	·	~q)	·	~(q	·	~p)
T	T	T		T		F	T	T		F
T	F	F		F		T	F	T		F
F	T	F		T		F	F	F		T
F	F	T		T		F	T	T		F

C. Basic Rules.

The rules I use follow fairly standard practice; but I do conceptualize some in terms of sign-changing rather than negation, and recognize some others in right- as well as left-hand mode. (I strictly bar right-hand Distribution, however, except to those who learned to read from right to left in early childhood. It generates errors, given the way our eyes track.) Specifically, I use simplification, conjunction, addition and disjunctive syllogism from both the right and the left, and Transposition, DeMorgan, and Material Implication in terms of sign changing. This avoids many tedious steps of commutation and double negation. Following your text and instructor, you may be playing a tighter game.

1. Basic Substitution (Equivalence) Rules. Truth tables show that certain expressions always share the same truth value. Substitution Rules allow us to exploit this by replacing such an expression with its mate.

Double Negation: Affirming is the same as denying denial.

$$p \equiv \sim\sim p$$

p	p	$\equiv$	$\sim\sim p$
T	T		T
F	T		F

Tautology: You need not repeat yourself; but you may if you like.

$$p \equiv (p \vee p)$$

p	p	$\equiv$	$(p \vee p)$
T	T		T
F	T		F

$$p \equiv (p \cdot p)$$

p	p	$\equiv$	$(p \cdot p)$
T	T		T
F	T		F

Commutation: Conjunctions and disjunctions may be turned around.

$$(p \vee q) \equiv (q \vee p)$$

p	q	$(p \vee q)$	$\equiv$	$(q \vee p)$
T	T	T	T	T
T	F	T	T	T
F	T	T	T	T
F	F	F	T	F

$(p \cdot q) \equiv (q \cdot p)$

p	q	$(p \cdot q)$	$\equiv$	$(q \cdot p)$
T	T	T	T	T
T	F	F	T	F
F	T	F	T	F
F	F	F	T	F

Association: How you group conjunct or disjunct strings depends on where you pause for breath.

$[p \cdot (q \cdot r)] \equiv [(p \cdot q) \cdot r]$ and $[p \vee (q \vee r)] \equiv [(p \vee q) \vee r]$

p	q	r	$[p \cdot$	$(q \cdot r)]$	$\equiv$	$[(p \cdot q)$	$\cdot r]$	$[p \vee$	$(q \vee r)]$	$\equiv$	$[(p \vee q)$	$\vee r]$
T	T	T	T	T	T	T	T	T	T	T	T	T
T	T	F	F	F	T	T	F	T	T	T	T	T
T	F	T	F	F	T	F	F	T	T	T	T	T
T	F	F	F	F	T	F	F	T	F	T	T	T
F	T	T	F	T	T	F	F	T	T	T	T	T
F	T	F	F	F	T	F	F	T	T	T	T	T
F	F	T	F	F	T	F	F	T	T	T	F	T
F	F	F	F	F	T	F	F	F	F	T	F	F

Distribution: "Multiplying through" isn't confined to arithmetic.

$[p \cdot (q \vee r)] \equiv [(p \cdot q) \vee (p \cdot r)]$ and
$[p \vee (q \cdot r)] \equiv [(p \vee q) \cdot (p \vee r)]$

p	q	r	$[p \cdot$	$(q \vee r)]$	$\equiv$	$[(p \cdot q)$	$\vee (p$	$\cdot r)]$
T	T	T	T	T	T	T	T	T
T	T	F	T	T	T	T	T	F
T	F	T	T	T	T	F	T	T
T	F	F	F	F	T	F	F	F
F	T	T	F	T	T	F	F	F
F	T	F	F	T	T	F	F	F
F	F	T	F	T	T	F	F	F
F	F	F	F	F	T	F	F	F

p	q	r	[p ∨ (q · r)]	≡	[(p ∨ q)	·	(p ∨ r)]
T	T	T	T T	T	T	T	T
T	T	F	T F	T	T	T	T
T	F	T	T F	T	T	T	T
T	F	F	T F	T	T	T	T
F	T	T	T T	T	T	T	T
F	T	F	F F	T	T	F	F
F	F	T	F F	T	F	F	T
F	F	F	F F	T	F	F	F

Exportation: Conditional antecedents can be lumped together or strung out.

[p ⊃ (q ⊃ r)] ≡ [(p · q) ⊃ r]

p	q	r	[p ⊃ (q ⊃ r)]	≡	[(p · q)	⊃ r]
T	T	T	T T	T	T	T
T	T	F	F F	T	T	F
T	F	T	T T	T	F	T
T	F	F	T T	T	F	T
F	T	T	T T	T	F	T
F	T	F	T F	T	F	T
F	F	T	T T	T	F	T
F	F	F	T T	T	F	T

Material Implication: A horseshoe can be replaced with a wedge (and vice versa) by changing the sign of the operator's antecedent. This rule (as well as the next two) is about the interchangeability of operators (which derives from the fact that all of them are defined in terms of dots and curls).

p ⊃ q) ≡ (~p ∨ q)

p	q	(p ⊃ q)	≡	(~p ∨ q)
T	T	T	T	T
T	F	F	T	F
F	T	T	T	T
F	F	T	T	T

(~p ⊃ q) ≡ (p ∨ q)

p	q	(~p ⊃ q)	≡	(p ∨ q)
T	T	T	T	T
T	F	T	T	T
F	T	T	T	T
F	F	F	T	F

Material Equivalence (A): A triple bar can be replaced with a set of horseshoes running both ways (and vice versa).

(p ≡ q) ≡ [(p ⊃ q) · (q ⊃ p)]

p q	(p ≡ q) ≡ [(p ⊃ q) · (q ⊃ p)]
T T	T T T T T
T F	F T F F T
F T	F T T F F
F F	T T T T T

De Morgan's Laws: A dot can be replaced by a wedge (and vice versa) if the signs of the compound and of both its components are changed.

~(p · q) ≡ (~p ∨ ~q)

p q	~(p · q) ≡ (~p ∨ ~q)
T T	F T T F
T F	T F T T
F T	T F T T
F F	T F T T

~(~p · ~q) ≡ (p ∨ q)

p q	~(~p · ~q) ≡ (p ∨ q)
T T	T F T T
T F	T F T T
F T	T F T T
F F	F T T F

~(~p ∨ ~q) ≡ (p · q)

p q	~(~p ∨ ~q) ≡ (p · q)
T T	T F T T
T F	F T T F
F T	F T T F
F F	F T T F

~(p ∨ q) ≡ (~p · ~q)

p q	~(p ∨ q) ≡ (~p · ~q)
T T	F T T F
T F	F T T F
F T	F T T F
F F	T F T T

2. Basic Inference Rules. Truth tables also show that certain argument are formed in such a way that whenever their premises are true their conclusions are true as well. Inference Rules allow us to take advantage of this by directly stating the conclusion of an argument of such form when its premises are given.

Simplification: A conjunction can be split up.

p · q /∴ p

p	q	p · q	/∴	p
T	T	T*		T*
T	F	F		T
F	T	F		F
F	F	F		F

p · q /∴ q

p	q	p · q	/∴	q
T	T	T*		T*
T	F	F		F
F	T	F		T
F	F	F		F

Conjunction: Individual propositions can be conjoined on one line.

p
q   /∴ p · q

p	q	p	q	/∴	p · q
T	T	T*	T*		T*
T	F	·T	F		F
F	T	F	T		F
F	F	F	F		F

Addition: Where p is true, a disjunction containing it will also be.

p /∴ p ∨ q

p	q	p	/∴	p ∨ q
T	T	T*		T*
T	F	T*		T*
F	T	F		T
F	F	F		F

p /∴ q ∨ p

p	q	p	/∴	q ∨ p
T	T	T*		T*
T	F	T*		T*
F	T	F		T
F	F	F		F

Modus Ponens: A true sufficient condition is enough.

p	q	p⊃q	p /∴	q
p ⊃ q				
p /∴ q				

p	q	p⊃q	p /∴	q
T	T	T*	T*	T*
T	F	F	T	F
F	T	T	F	T
F	F	T	F	F

Absorption: Trivial-appearing (and redundant once Conditional Proof is in place); but useful for generating tautologies.

p ⊃ q /∴ p ⊃ (p · q)

p	q	p⊃q	/∴ p ⊃ (p · q)	
T	T	T*	T*	T
T	F	F	F	F
F	T	T*	T*	F
F	F	T*	T*	F

D. Derived Rules.

Using these basic substitution and inference rules, we can deductively establish several additional rules which, when used, make our proofs shorter. (With infinitely many rules, no proof would involve the citation of more than one.)

1.   Derived Substitution Rules. There are two additional common substitution rules that I will not show on truth tables. They could be; but they can also be conditionally proven using only the inference and substitution rules that have already been shown. I will demonstrate this when I explain Conditional Proof itself.

Material Equivalence (B): Since triple bars go to horseshoes which go to wedges which go to dots, why not do it all at once?

(p ≡ q) ≡ [(p · q) ∨ (~p · ~q)]

Transposition: A horseshoe's antecedent and consequent can be swapped by changing the signs of both.

(p ⊃ q) ≡ (~q ⊃ ~p)

2. Derived Inference Rules. There are also five common inference rules that I will not show on truth tables. They could be, too; but they can also be proven using only the inference and substitution rules that have already been shown.

Modus Tollens: The lack of a necessary condition is enough. (Modus Ponens for negative thinkers.)

1. p ⊃ q		
2. ~q	/∴	**~p**
3. ~p ∨ q	1	Material Implication
4. q ∨ ~p	3	Commutation
5. ~q ⊃ ~p	4	Material Implication
6. ~p	5,2	Modus Ponens

Disjunctive Syllogism: Process of elimination.

1. p ∨ q		
2. ~p	/∴	**q**
3. ~p ⊃ q	1	Material Implication
4. q	3,2	Modus Ponens

1. p ∨ q		
2. ~q	/∴	**p**
3. q ∨ p	1	Commutation
4. ~q ⊃ p	3	Material Implication
5. p	4,2	Modus Ponens

Constructive Dilemma: Using the debaters' rule saves fourteen steps.

1. (p ⊃ q) · (r ⊃ s)		
2. p ∨ r	/∴	**q ∨ s**
3. (~p ∨ q) · (~r ∨ s)	1	Material Implication
4. ~p ∨ q	3	Simplification
5. ~r ∨ s	3	Simplification
6. (~p ∨ q) ∨ s	4	Addition
7. ~p ∨ (q ∨ s)	6	Association
8. (~r ∨ s) ∨ q	5	Addition
9. ~r ∨ (s ∨ q)	8	Association
10. ~r ∨ (q ∨ s)	9	Commutation

11. [~p ∨ (q ∨ s)] · [~r ∨ (q ∨ s)]	7,10	Conjunction
12. [(q ∨ s) ∨ ~p] · [(q ∨ s) ∨ ~r]	11	Commutation
13. (q ∨ s) ∨ (~p · ~r)	12	Distribution
14. (~p · ~r) ∨ (q ∨ s)	13	Commutation
15. ~(p ∨ r) ∨ (q ∨ s)	14	De Morgan
16. (p ∨ r) ⊃ (q ∨ s)	15	Material Implication
17. q ∨ s	16,2	Modus Ponens

Destructive Dilemma: Negative debaters' rule. With a small amount of shuffling, this can be derived by Constructive Dilemma, already derived itself. Thus twice redundant, it is often omitted from the lists.

1. (p ⊃ q) · (r ⊃ s)		
2. ~q ∨ ~s	/∴	**~p ∨ ~r**
3. (~p ∨ q) · (~r ∨ s)	1	Material Implication
4. (q ∨ ~p) · (s ∨ ~r)	3	Commutation
5. (~q ⊃ ~p) · (~s ⊃ ~r)	4	Material Implication
6. ~p ∨ ~r	5,2	Constructive Dilemma

Hypothetical Syllogism: Chain argument. A dilemma without a disjunction provided. Since the needed one is a tautology, absorption unlocks the door.

1. p ⊃ q		
2. q ⊃ r	/∴	**p ⊃ r**
3. q ⊃ (q · r)	2	Absorption
4. ~q ∨ (q · r)	3	Material Implication
5. (~q ∨ q) · (~q ∨ r)	4	Distribution
6. ~q ∨ q	5	Simplification
7. ~p ∨ q	1	Material Implicatio
8. q ∨ ~p	7	Commutation
9. ~q ⊃ ~p	8	Material Implication
10. (~q ⊃ ~p) · (q ⊃ r)	9,2	Conjunction
11. ~p ∨ r	10,6	Constructive Dilemma
12. p ⊃ r	11	Material Implication

Since Constructive Dilemma is a derived rule itself, an even more thorough derivation is possible for chaining.

1. p ⊃ q		
2. q ⊃ r	/∴	p ⊃ r
3. p ⊃ (p · q)	1	Absorption
4. ~p ∨ (p · q)	3	Material Implication
5. (~p ∨ p) · (~p · q)	4	Distribution
6. ~p ∨ p	5	Simplification
7. (~p ∨ p) ∨ r	6	Addition
8. ~p ∨ (p ∨ r)	7	Association
9. ~p ∨ (r ∨ p)	8	Commutation
10. (~p ∨ r) ∨ p	9	Association
11. ~q ∨ r	2	Material Implication
12. r ∨ ~q	11	Commutation
13. ~p ∨ (r ∨ ~q)	12	Addition
14. (~p ∨ r) ∨ ~q	13	Association
15. [(~p ∨ r) ∨ p] · [(~p ∨ r) ∨ ~q	10,14	Conjunction
16. (~p ∨ r) ∨ (p · ~q)	5	Distribution
17. ~p ∨ q	1	Material Implication
18. ~(p · ~q)	17	De Morgan
19. ~p ∨ r	16,18	Disjunctive Syllogism
20. p ⊃ r	19	Material Implication

E. Conditional Proofs.

I will use Conditional (including Reductio ad Absurdum or Indirect) Proofs from time to time. While many texts rely on them heavily, exclusive or premature reliance on such techniques avoids some of the manipulations that a beginning student should learn to carry out. So some texts banish them from the introductory scene completely. In my own view, they are too powerful to ignore, but dulling if overused. Knowing that individual instructors will use their own judgement about what to allow (and when), I have often provided more than one solution.

While conditional techniques often make proof construction shorter and simpler, they can neither be demonstrated on a truth table nor inferred from rules that can. One kind of truth table will show the validity status of an argument. Another kind will show the truth status of a proposition. A truth table for a conditional proof would need to show that a particular argument, taken as a whole, is equivalent to a particular conditional tautology. But there is no operator in the system for that kind of equivalence. Nor can one truth table accommodate both the argument

and the proposition that would have to go on either side of the non-exis-
tent operator. The propriety of the technique can, nevertheless, be shown
discursively.

1. Basic Conditional Proof Technique.

In essence, constructing any formal proof amounts to demonstrating
that some output or other can be derived from one or more assumptions
in a finite number of legal steps. Most common instances of such proof
use the premises of an argument as the assumptions and its conclusion as
the output. For example:

p ⊃ q
p   /∴   q

1. p ⊃ q   assumption (premise 1)
2. p   assumption (premise 2)
3. q   output (conclusion)
                                    from 1 and 2 by Modus Ponens

This demonstrates that the argument is valid: the output (conclusion)
can be derived from the assumptions (premises) in a finite number of
steps (one) by the use of justified rule(s). But the method can also be ap-
plied to a conditional statement, taking its antecedent as the assumption
and its consequent as the output. For example:

                                    /∴   [(p ⊃ q) · p] ⊃ q

1. (p ⊃ q) · p   assumption (antecedent)
2. p ⊃ q   from 1 by Simplification
3. p   from 1 by Simplification
4. q   output (consequent)
                                    from 2 and 3 by Modus Ponens

This demonstrates that the conditional proposition is true: the output
(consequent) can be derived from the assumption (antecedent) in a finite
number of steps (three) by the use of justified rule(s).

We could use formal proof technique to demonstrate the truth of many
other true implications. Here are just two more:

$/\therefore \quad p \supset (q \supset p)$

1. p	assumption (antecedent)
2. ~q ∨ p	from 1 by Addition
3. q ⊃p	output (consequent)
	from 2 by Material Implication

$/\therefore \quad (p \equiv q) \supset (p \supset q)$

1. p ≡ q	assumption (antecedent)
2. (p ⊃ q) · (q ⊃ p)	from 1 by Material Equivalence (A)
3. p ⊃ q	output (consequent)
	from 2 by Simplification

Certain conventions are followed when such proofs are written out. The assumption or hypothesis (the antecedent of the conditional we are trying to prove to be true) is marked by a trailing marginal bracket to its left which extends to include the output (the consequent of the conditional sought). The hypothesis must be discharged, for reasons that I will state shortly. The fact that it is not left hanging is noted by bending its trailing bracket back across the body of the proof when the desired output has been established on its basis. Finally, a further line is added (immediately following the discharge of the hypothesis). It always consists of a conditional statement the antecedent of which is the hypothesis itself, and the consequent of which is the immediately preceding line (what has been derived on the basis of the assumption). This added line says in one string what has just been carried out in the body of the derivation: the assumption of the antecedent leads to the consequent. Finally, this line is justified by reference to all the lines used in the written inference from antecedent to consequent, and is labelled "Conditional Proof."

Following these conventions, the immediately previous formal proofs of three true conditionals would be written as follows:

$/\therefore \ [(p \supset q) \cdot p] \supset q$

1. (p ⊃ q) · p		
2. p ⊃ q	1	Simplification
3. p	1	Simplification
4. q	2,3	Modus Ponens
5. [(p ⊃ q) · p] ⊃ q	1-4	Conditional Proof

$/\therefore$ p ⊃ (q ⊃ p)

```
┌  1. p
│  2. ~q ∨ p          1      Addition
└  3. q ⊃p            2      Material Implication
   4. p ⊃ (q ⊃ p)     1-3    Conditional Proof
```

$/\therefore$ (p ≡ q) ⊃ (p ⊃ q)

```
┌  1. p ≡ q
│  2. (p ⊃ q) · (q ⊃ p)    1      Material Equivalence (A)
└  3. p ⊃ q                2      Simplification
   4. (p ≡ q) ⊃ (p ⊃ q)    1-3    Conditional Proof
```

Such conditional proofs clearly demonstrate that the conditional statements on their last lines are true. They do not demonstrate the truth of any of their internal lines, however. Those internal lines all fall within the scope of the hypothesis drawn, and (as such) can be inferred to be true only if the hypothesis itself is true. That is why hypotheses must be discharged. Nothing follows from a conditional proof except a conditional statement.

One can assume any hypothesis whatever. If an hypothesis 'p' generates any output 'q', then 'p ⊃ q' will have been shown to be a true implication statement. This can be fruitfully exploited. For example:

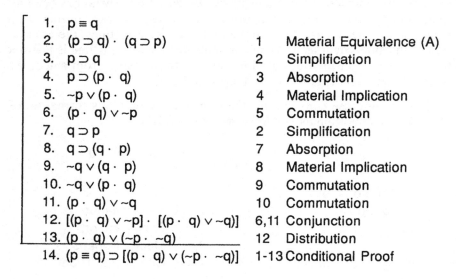

```
┌  1.  p ≡ q
│  2.  (p ⊃ q) · (q ⊃ p)                      1       Material Equivalence (A)
│  3.  p ⊃ q                                  2       Simplification
│  4.  p ⊃ (p · q)                            3       Absorption
│  5.  ~p ∨ (p · q)                           4       Material Implication
│  6.  (p · q) ∨ ~p                           5       Commutation
│  7.  q ⊃ p                                  2       Simplification
│  8.  q ⊃ (q · p)                            7       Absorption
│  9.  ~q ∨ (q · p)                           8       Material Implication
│  10. ~q ∨ (p · q)                           9       Commutation
│  11. (p · q) ∨ ~q                           10      Commutation
│  12. [(p · q) ∨ ~p] · [(p · q) ∨ ~q)]       6,11    Conjunction
└  13. (p · q) ∨ (~p · ~q)                    12      Distribution
   14. (p ≡ q) ⊃ [(p · q) ∨ (~p · ~q)]        1-13    Conditional Proof
```

```
┌  15.  (p · q) ] ∨ (~p · ~q)
│  16.  [(p · q) ∨ ~p] · [(p · q) ∨ ~q)]    15      Distribution
│  17.  (p · q) ∨ ~q                        16      Simplification
│  18.  ~q ∨ (p · q)                        17      Commutation
│  19.  (~q ∨ p) · (~q ∨ q)                 18      Distribution
│  20.  ~q ∨ p                              19      Simplification
│  21.  (p · q) ∨ ~p                        16      Simplification
│  22.  ~p ∨ (p · q)                        21      Commutation
│  23.  (~p ∨ p) · (~p ∨ q)                 22      Distribution
│  24.  ~p ∨ q                              23      Simplification
│  25.  (~p ∨ q) · (~q ∨ p)                 24,20   Conjunction
│  26.  (p ⊃ q) · (q ⊃ p)                   25      Material Implication
└  27.  p ≡ q                               26      Material Equivalence (A)
   28.  [(p · q) ∨ (~p · ~q)] ⊃ (p ≡ q)     15-27   Conditional Proof
   29.  {(p ≡ q) ⊃ [(p · q) ∨ (~p · ~q)]} · {[(p · q) ∨ (~p · ~q)] ⊃ (p ≡ q)}
                                            14,28   Conjunction
   30.  (p ≡ q) ≡ [(p · q) ∨ (~p · ~q)]     29      Material Equivalence (A)
```

Thus, conditional proof allows a complete derivation of the substitution rule **Material Equivalence (B)**. It does the same for **Transposition** as well:

```
┌  1.  p ⊃ q
│  2.  ~p ∨ q                               1       Material Implication
│  3.  q ∨ ~p                               2       Commutation
└  4.  ~q ⊃ ~p                              3       Material Implication
   5.  (p ⊃ q) ⊃ (~q ⊃ ~p)                  1-4     Conditional Proof
┌  6.  ~q ⊃ ~p
│  7.  q ∨ ~p                               6       Material Implication
│  8.  ~p ∨ q                               7       Commutation
└  9.  p ⊃ q                                8       Material Implication
   10. (~q ⊃ ~p) ⊃ (p ⊃ q)                  6-10    Conditional Proof
   11. [(p ⊃ q) ⊃ (~q ⊃ ~p)] · [(~q ⊃ ~p) ⊃ (p ⊃ q)]
                                            5,10    Conjunction
   12. (p ⊃ q) ≡ (~q ⊃ ~p)                  11      Material Equivalence (A)
```

2. Using Conditional Proof in Ordinary Settings

It should be obvious that any argument whatever can be rewritten as a conditional statement (and vice versa). Exchange the premise (or a conjunction of them if there are more than one) with the antecedent, exchange the conclusion with the consequent, and exchange the 'therefore' with a horseshoe. Saying, "if p then q," and saying, "on the assumption 'p,' 'q' follows," are just two ways of saying the same thing. They can both be formally proven (one valid, the other true), as shown above, and there is no difference between the proofs except for the arrangement of the lines. They are interchangeable. This, too, can be exploited. Consider two further arguments:

A.	1. (p ∨ q) ⊃ r	/∴	p ⊃ r
	2. ~(p ∨ q) ∨ r	1	Material Implication
	3. (~p · ~q) ∨ r	2	De Morgan
	4. r ∨ (~p · ~q)	3	Commutation
	5. (r ∨ ~p) · (r ∨ ~q)	4	Distribution
	6. r ∨ ~p	5	Simplification
	7. ~p ∨ r	6	Commutation
	8. p ⊃ r	7	Material Implication

B.	1. (p ∨ q) ⊃ r		
	2. p	/∴	r
	3. p ∨ q	2	Addition
	4. r	1,3	Modus Ponens

Arguments A and B, of course, are equivalent (respectively) to the two tautological conditional statements:

a. [(p ∨ q) ⊃ r] ⊃ (p ⊃ r);

b. {[(p ∨ q) ⊃ r] · p} ⊃ r.

And these two conditionals are equivalent to each other by the substitution rule Exportation:

{[(p ∨ q) ⊃ r] ⊃ (p ⊃ r)} ≡ ({[(p ∨ q) ⊃ r] · p} ⊃ r)

Here is where the **Law of Transitive Equivalence** comes into play. If each of the two arguments is equivalent to one of two conditional statements (A is equivalent to a, and B is equivalent to b), and a and b are equivalent to each other, then the arguments A and B are themselves equivalent to each other too. Once we recognize the equivalence of the two arguments, a new application of conditional proof is both obvious and attractive.

So, let us return to argument A, but hypothesize the antecedent of its conclusion so as to run a conditional proof within it:

A'.   1. **(p ∨ q) ⊃ r**   /∴   **p ⊃ r**

2. p		
3. p ∨ q	2	Addition
4. r	1,3	Modus Ponens
5. p ⊃ r	2-4	Conditional Proof

In effect, this replaces the more complex of the two original arguments with its easier equivalent (which has an extra premise and a shorter conclusion to prove). A highly economical move; and conditional technique almost always provides such economies when working on arguments that have a conditional conclusion. It is also helpful with arguments with conclusions which, while not conditionals as such, can be restated in some conditional form. Here are two examples:

1. **p ⊃ (q · w)**		
2. **q ⊃ r**	/∴	**~(p · ~r)**
3. p		
4 q · w	1,3	Modus Ponens
5. q	4	Simplification
6. r	2,5	Modus Ponens
7. p ⊃ r	3-6	Conditional Proof
8. ~p ∨ r	7	Material Implication
9. ~(p · ~r)	8	De Morgan

1. **p ⊃ (q · w)**		
2. **(q ∨ s) ⊃ p**	/∴	**p ≡ q**
3. p		
4. q · w	1,3	Modus Ponens
5. q	4	Simplification
6. p ⊃ q	3-5	Conditional Proof

7. q		
8. q ∨ s	7	Addition
9. p	2,8	Modus Ponens
10. q ⊃ p	7-9	Conditional Proof
11. (p ⊃ q) · (q ⊃ p)	6,10	Conjunction
12. p ≡ q	11	Material Equivalence (A)

Such economies are why too much conditional proof is counterproductive. (One really does need to know how to do things like distribute and simplify.) Nevertheless, the manoeuvre is legitimate, given the Law of Transitive Equivalence, because of the clear legitimacy of conditional proof for establishing the truth of implication statements.

3.   A Special Application of Conditional Proof

One further useful application of conditional proof is the construction of Indirect or "Reductio ad Absurdum" Proofs. Those who know their Euclid are familiar with this line of argument, but may not realize that it is just an application of the general conditional technique.

Reductio proof amounts to hypothesizing the denial of the conclusion which is sought, and showing that this hypothesis leads directly to inconsistency. If a hypothesis entails absurdities, then the hypothesis must be false. So, in this case, the denial of what you are trying to establish is false. So, by the law of contradiction, what you are trying to establish is true. QED. Here is an example which strictly follows the conventions for Conditional Proof:

1. p ⊃ q		
2. p	/∴	q
3. ~q		
4. ~p	1,3	Modus Tollens
5. p · ~p	2,4	Conjunction
6. ~q ⊃ (p · ~p)	3-5	Conditional Proof
7. q ∨ (p · ~p)	6	Material Implication
8. (q ∨ p) · (q ∨ ~p)	7	Distribution
9. q ∨ p	8	Simplification
10. ~q ⊃ p	9	Material Implication
11. ~q ⊃ q	10,1	Hypothetical Syllogism
12. q ∨ q	11	Material Implication
13. q	12	Tautology

Any Indirect Proof can be written out in full this way. If one does so, the last nine lines always have the same form: first a contradiction, then a conditional statement (that the hypothesis implies the contradiction), etc. Consequently, there is a well established convention which allows one to replace the last eight lines with a summary justificatory line, allowing the whole argument to be written as follows:

1. $p \supset q$
2. p $/\therefore$ q
3. $\sim q$
4. $\sim p$ 1,3   Modus Tollens
5. $p \cdot \sim p$ 2,4   Conjunction
6. q 3-5   Reductio ad Absurdum

Every time Reductio Ad Absurdum is cited, one should understand that seven additional lines of a strict conditional proof are on tap. This way of writing it is only shorthand.

F. Quantification.

I use normal procedures for generalizing and instantiating propositions in the process of running quantified proofs. These procedures cannot, of course, be proved on finite truth tables, nor can they be derived from any more basic formal procedures. They constitute, then, five more basic rules (axioms, postulates, conventions) for the system. Using 'P' as a property variable, 'x' as an individual variable (of either open or limited domain), 'n' as a place marker for an individual constant, and 'y' as the name of that individual (if there is one) which has all and only those properties which all individuals possess, these quantification procedures can be stated as follows:

Quantifier Negation. The denial of a universal assertion is the assertion of a particular denial, and the denial of a particular assertion is the assertion of a universal denial.

$$\sim(x)Px \equiv (\exists x)\sim Px \text{ and } \sim(\exists x)Px \equiv (x)\sim Px$$

Universal Instantiation. A property which is true of everything is true of any individual you choose.

$$(x)Px \qquad\qquad /\therefore \quad Pn$$

Existential Generalization. A property which is true of an individual is true of some individual or other.

    Pn   /∴ **(∃x)Px**

Existential Instantiation. An individual, identified only by the possession of a property, may be given a name for purposes of reference, as long as that name has no prior use in the context, and is un-universalizable.

    (∃x)Px   /∴ **Pn**

[Restriction: The name here represented by the marker 'n' must be a constant (other than y) without prior use in the argument. The reason for this restriction is to prevent any unwarranted assumption either a) that multiple existential assertions have the same subject, or b) that y has a property which only some individuals have.]

Universal Generalization. One very restricted constant may be universally generalized.

    Py   /∴ **(x)Px**

[Restriction: 'y' can be introduced into the argument only by Universal Instantiation or by hypothesis as part of a conditional proof. The reason for this restriction is to prevent universalizing any properties which belong only to a limited number of individuals. It works because if 'y' has been introduced into the argument by instantiating a universal statement in the first place, we are only re-universalizing what was universal already; and if it has been introduced by way of hypothesis in a conditional proof, it will yield only conditional statements for output. Even with its restrictions, some may find that Universal Generalization looks too much like "Converse Accident" for comfort. To avoid even the semblance of evil, one can prove all arguments that have universal conclusions by Reductio. Then Universal Generalization will never come into play.]

The exercises in this book that involve quantifiers are all singly general. *No* relations are involved. Occasionally, restricting the domain of the variable (specifying a value for x) will simplify matters. When such a restriction (usually to "persons") is obvious, it is left implicit. Otherwise, I have stated it.

G. Invalidity.

I have provided fewer invalid arguments here than one is likely to find in the real world, trusting symbolization errors to bring the ratio up to normal. One should always be alert to the possibility of invalidity. Few things are more frustrating than the discovery that an argument is invalid after many futile hours of earnest attempts at proof. Invalidity, of course, has to be shown by some sort of truth table apparatus. For propositional arguments, this can be done by constructing a complete table; but if the argument has very many components, this is not practical. I have, consequently, followed the standard practice of constructing (by trial and error) a single line from such a table which shows all the premises true and the conclusion false. Life is more complicated when working with quantified arguments. Complete truth tables are impossible rather than impractical, for they would have to be multiply infinite in size, with infinitely many instantiations in the column for each line of the argument. Consquently, I fall back on assigning truth values in a manageable (but fictitious) finite universe of n individuals. This does not show invalidity only for the constructed universe. Invalidity for a universe of n individuals can be discursively shown to infect a universe of n plus 1 individuals. So, invalidity follows, *seriatim*, for any and all universes larger than n.

H. A Summary Statement of the Rules.

SUBSTITUTION RULES

Double Negation [DN]:	$p \equiv \sim\sim p$
Tautology [Taut]:	$p \equiv (p \vee p)$
	$p \equiv (p \cdot p)$
Commutation [Com]:	$(p \vee q) \equiv (q \vee p)$
	$(p \cdot q) \equiv (q \cdot p)$
Material Implication [MI]:	$(p \supset q) \equiv (\sim p \vee q)$
	$(\sim p \supset q) \equiv (p \vee q)$

Transposition [Transp]:	$(p \supset q) \equiv (\sim q \supset \sim p)$
Association [Assc]:	$[p \cdot (q \cdot r)] \equiv [(p \cdot q) \cdot r]$
	$[p \vee (q \vee r)] \equiv [(p \vee q) \vee r]$
Exportation [Export]:	$[p \supset (q \supset r)] \equiv [(p \cdot q) \supset r]$
Distribution [Dist]	$[p \cdot (q \vee r)] \equiv [(p \cdot q) \vee (p \cdot r)]$
	$[p \vee (q \cdot r)] \equiv [(p \vee q) \cdot (p \vee r)]$
De Morgan [DeM]:	$\sim(p \cdot q) \equiv (\sim p \vee \sim q)$
	$\sim(\sim p \cdot \sim q) \equiv (p \vee q)$
	$\sim(p \vee q) \equiv (\sim p \cdot \sim q)$
	$\sim(\sim p \vee \sim q) \equiv (p \cdot q)$
Material Equivalence A (MEA):	$(p \equiv q) \equiv [(p \supset q) \cdot (q \supset p)]$
Material Equivalence B (MEB):	$(p \equiv q) \equiv [(p \cdot q) \vee (\sim p \cdot \sim q)]$

INFERENCE RULES

Simplification [Simp]:	$p \cdot q$	$/\therefore p$
	$p \cdot q$	$/\therefore q$
Conjunction [Conj]:	p	
	q	$/\therefore p \cdot q$
Addition [Add]:	p	$/\therefore p \vee q$
	p	$/\therefore q \vee p$
Modus Ponens [MP]:	$p \supset q$	
	p	$/\therefore q$

Modus Tollens [MT]:

$p \supset q$
$\sim q$ $\quad / \therefore \sim p$

Absorption [Abs]:

$p \supset q$ $\quad / \therefore p \supset (p \cdot q)$

Disjunctive Syllogism [DS]:

$p \vee q$
$\sim p$ $\quad / \therefore q$

$p \vee q$
$\sim q$ $\quad / \therefore p$

Constructive Dilemma [CD]:

$(p \supset q) \cdot (r \supset s)$
$p \vee r$ $\quad / \therefore q \vee s$

Hypothetical Syllogism [HS]:

$p \supset q$
$q \supset r$ $\quad / \therefore p \supset r$

Basic Conditional Proof (CP):

$$\begin{array}{|l}
p \\
\cdot \\
\cdot \\
\underline{q} \\
\end{array}$$
$p \supset q$

Reductio Proof (RAA):

$$\begin{array}{|l}
p \\
\cdot \\
\cdot \\
\underline{q \cdot \sim q} \\
\end{array}$$
$\sim p$

QUANTIFICATION RULES

Quantifier Negation [QN]:

$$\sim(x)Px \equiv (\exists x)\sim Px$$

$$\sim(\exists x)Px \equiv (x)\sim Px$$

Existential Instantiation [EI]:   (∃x)Px   /∴ **Pn**

[Restriction: The name represented by the marker 'n' must be a constant (other than y) without prior use in the argument.]

Existential Generalization [EG]:   **Pn**   /∴ (∃x)**Px**

Universal Instantiation [UI]:   **(x)Px**   /∴ **Pn**

Universal Generalization [UG]:   **Py**   /∴ **(x)Px**

[Restriction: 'y' can be introduced into the argument only by Universal Instantiation or by hypothesis as part of a conditional proof.]

TWO: SENTENTIAL PROBLEMS

A: EASY PROBLEMS.

1. Bill will pass Logic 101 if and only if he does his homework. If doing his homework is a sufficient condition of Bill's passing Logic 101 then it must not be a very hard course. So Logic 101 is not a very hard course. (P,W,H)

2. This problem is too hard for Clyde if and only if he did not do yesterday's homework. He did not do that homework. So this problem is too hard for him unless he cheats. (H,W,C)

3. Either inflation will stop or meat will become so expensive that only the rich can afford it. If meat becomes that expensive, college teachers will become vegetarians out of financial necessity. Inflation isn't going to stop; and if college teachers are forced by economic pressures to give up eating meat, we can expect unionization on the college and university front soon. It follows that it will not be long until such schools unionize. (I,M,T,U)

4. Anacin and Bufferin cannot both be the best analgesic on the market. So if Bufferin is, then Anacin isn't. (A,B)

5. This is either real sherry or else it is a fortified wine and is mixed with flavorings. If it is real sherry then it is a fortified wine. It is bottled in Jerex if and only if it is real sherry. If it is bottled in Jerex it is not Thunderbird. Therefore, it is not Thunderbird if and only if it is real sherry. (S,F,M,J,T)

6. If they keep digging in Westhampton Green for another week, they will find oil there. Oil will be found in Westhampton Green only if there are some known geological dome structures in the Richmond area. Geologists would have thoroughly mapped Richmond if there were any known geological dome structures there. Geologists have never thoroughly mapped Richmond. So the digging in Westhampton Green will stop before the week is out. (D,F,K,M)

7. If I eat pizza I will have indigestion. I will either eat pizza or lasagna. If I eat lasagna, I would be eating something with riccota cheese in it. I would never eat anything with riccota cheese in it. So, I will eat pizza and have indigestion. (P,I,L,R)

8. Neither donuts nor Twinkies are nutritious. If donuts are not nutritious, then Bubba's eating habits are bad. Bubba's eating habits are OK if he is on the meal plan. So Bubba is not on the meal plan. (D,T,B,M)

9. If I don't study I will make bad grades. If I do study, I will not have any fun. So it is either bad grades or no fun for me. (S,B,F)

10. A thermal inversion means stagnant air. The air isn't stagnant without there being a risk of dangerous smog. There isn't a risk of dangerous smog unless the carbon disulfide level hovers about 2%. So, where there is a thermal inversion the carbon disulfide level hovers about 2%. (T,S,R,C)

11. Only if Dr. Jones is called out on an emergency, will she be unable to treat her regular patients on time. But she must either treat them on time or lose some of them. Therefore, if she is not called out on an emergency, she will not lose any of her regular patients. (E,T,L)

12. If you feed the lawn it will grow. If you feed the lawn, then if it grows, it will have to be cut. Feeding the lawn means that it has to be cut if and only if there is plenty of sun. Therefore, if there is plenty of sun and the lawn has to be cut, you must have fed the lawn. (F,G,C,S)

13. If you make over 75 you will pass. If you do not cheat you will not pass. Either you make over 75 or you will not pass. So you will make over 75 if and only if you cheat. (O, P, C)

14. I will pass Calculus III if and only if I score 95 or better on the final exam. I will not score that well on the exam unless a miracle of some kind occurs. If it is true that I will pass Calculus III only if there is a miracle of some kind, then my chances of passing it are poor. So I have a poor chance of passing Calculus III. (C,S,M,P)

15. If this is April, then if the begonias are blooming now, then Spring will end early this year. Begonias are blooming now if and only if the last day of frost was in February. Spring will not end early this year unless the last day of frost was in February. So the last day of frost was in February if and only if Spring is short this year. (A,B,S,L)

16. If the Prince Consort is lecherous then the royal family will be

upset. The Prince Consort is either lecherous or else the press is being unfair. The press clearly is not being unfair. So the royal family is going to be upset. (L,U,F)

17. The Russians will accept our proposal for banning chemical warfare only if we drop our demand for on-site inspections. The U.S. will drop that demand if and only if we believe everything the Russians tell us. We will not believe everything the Russians tell us unless we are incredibly naive. So, if we are incredibly naive and drop our demand for on-site inspections, the Russians will accept our proposal for banning chemical warfare. (A,D,B,N)

18. Coming to class is enough to get a D or better. If you come to class, then if you get D or better then the instructor must be lenient. Coming to class will get you a D or better if and only if the course is a gut course. Therefore if the course is a gut course and the instructor is lenient, then you will get a D or better. (C,D,L,G)

19. If we get out of Saudi Arabia, Iraq will surely take over that country; but if we don't get out, our men will continue getting killed in a frustrating and pointless war. Our men are not going to continue getting killed in those circumstances. So it is clear that Iraq is going to take over there. (O,T,K)

20. If this is Monday I have both a Literature exam and an Economics exam today. If I have a Literature exam today, I will be writing non-stop for three hours. So I will be writing non-stop for three hours if this is Monday. (M,L,E,W)

21. If today is Monday, I have Logic. Today is either Monday or Tuesday. If today is Tuesday, I have a council meeting. I have no council meeting today. Therefore I do have Logic today. (M,L,T,C)

22. Paul will not pass logic unless he studies it. Paul will not study logic. If Paul is enrolled in logic, then if he doesn't pass it he will flunk it. So, if Paul is enrolled in logic, he will flunk it. (P,S,E,F)

23. If the supply of crude oil goes down 60%, then the price of crude oil will triple. But either that price will not triple or else gasoline will go over $2.00 a gallon. But gasoline will go over $2.00 a gallon if and only if the government deregulates. So, if either the supply of crude oil goes down 60% or if demand for it increases by half, then the government will deregulate. (S,P,O,G,D)

24. Franks are fattening unless they are boiled. Franks are greasy only if they are not boiled. If franks are not fattening only if they are not greasy, then my new diet is going to be dull. My new diet will not be dull unless I am serious about losing weight. Therefore I am serious about losing weight. (F,B,G,D,S)

25. If we don't invade Canada the Communists will surely take over that country; but if we do, then American soldiers will be killed there. So, either the Communists will take over Canada or American soldiers will be killed there. (I,C,K)

26. My tulips are doomed unless I prepared the soil and used bone meal. If my tulips are doomed unless I used bone meal, then my garden will be drab in the Spring. My garden will not be drab in the Spring unless I am lazy. So I must be lazy. (D,P,B,G,L)

27. If it snows in March then the Spring water table will be high. My azaleas will bloom well if and only if there is a high Spring water table. A fine bloom on my azaleas will be enough to make my house look good. I will find a buyer for my house if it looks good. Therefore, if it snows in March I will find a buyer for my house. (S,W,A,G,B)

28. Iran will release the hostages only if Kelly is more forceful than North and Bush lets Kelly have his own way. If Iran does not release the hostages or if Bush does let Kelly have his own way, then trade restrictions will be counter-productive. Trade restrictions are not counter-productive unless traditional diplomacy is utterly useless. So traditional diplomacy must be utterly useless (I,K,B,T,U)

B: MEDIUM PROBLEMS.

29. Validity is a matter of form, and our two arguments have the same form. If all this is so, then your argument is valid if and only if mine is valid. My argument has true premises and false conclusion. It cannot have true premises and false conclusion and still be valid. So your argument is not valid. (F,S,Y,M,T)

30. Greece will reject the exchange unless both Nicholas and Miller are double agents. Although Nicholas is a double agent only if Miller is not, Athens is nevertheless a hotbed of espionage. If either Whitehall or the Kremlin gets it way, then Greece will not reject the exchange. If neither Whitehall nor the Kremlin gets its way, then subversive elements in Greece will be reduced. Therefore that reduction will take place. (G,N, M,A,W,K,S)

31. If Olga can do the homework she will pass the test. If Olga can do the homework, then if she passes the test she will pass the course. It is not the case that Olga's ability to do the homework is a sufficient condition of her passing the course unless the course is too easy for her. It is too easy for Olga only if either a) she has covered the material previously or b) she has a natural flair for problem solving. Olga has not covered the material before. So, Olga does have a natural flair for problem solving. (H,T,C,E,P,N)

32. John is a success if and only if he married money. He is not a success; but his wife is independently wealthy. Therefore Sam should have intervened. (J,M,S)

33. The tulips will bloom only if there is a large quantity of sunshine. Either the tulips will bloom or else April will be colder than normal and the ground will remain wet. The claim that April will be colder than normal unless smog produces a greenhouse effect is a false claim. Nitrogen will accumulate in the soil if the ground remains wet. So, either there will be a large quantity of sunshine or nitrogen will accumulate in the soil. (T,Q,A,W,S,N)

34. The invasion will fail unless Aberystwyth is taken. But Aberystwyth will be taken only if Harlech falls. Further, the King will flee into exile if the invasion fails. Therefore, Harlech will fall unless the King flees into exile. (I,A,H,K)

35. If you like pastrami or corned beef you will like the New York Deli. So, if you like corned beef you will like either the New York Deli or Bernie's. (P,C,N,B)

36. They went out for supper or for cocktails and dancing. If they went out for cocktails, then if they went dancing, then they had a nice evening. It is false that they had a nice evening and went out for supper. So they did not have a nice evening if and only if they went out for supper. (S,C,D,N)

37. If I eat pizza I'll get heartburn; and if I eat anchovies, I'll have bad breath. So if I eat pizza with anchovies, I'll have heartburn and bad breath. (P,H,A,B)

38. If you enroll in the course and study hard you will pass; but if you enroll in the course and do not study hard you will not pass. Therefore, if you enroll in the course, you will either study hard and pass or not study hard and not pass. (E,S,P)

39. I will not understand the questions unless I translate them, and if I am to succeed, then I must understand them. Therefore, I will receive the prize and succeed only if I translate the questions. (U,T,S,P)

40. If you can subtract then you can divide; and if you can subtract then if you can divide then you can extract roots. But if the ability to subtract implies the ability to extract roots, then any bright second grader can extract roots. It is true that any bright second grader can extract roots if and only if radicals are very easy. It follows that radicals are very easy. (S,D,E,B,R)

41. If I take ancient Sanskrit I will fail it. If I am going to make either an F or a D in ancient Sanskrit, then I will not take the course. I can win the Boatwright Prize only if I take both Homer and ancient Sanskrit. I will win the Boatwright Prize. So I must have bribed the prize committee. (S,F,D,W,H,B)

42. If you took music appreciation you made an A; and if you took sociology you made an A. If you made an A your mother will be proud of you. So, if your mother is not proud of you, you didn't take music appreciation or sociology. (M,A,S,P)

43. Aaron will pass only if he lies or cheats. If Aaron cheats, then if the proctor observes it, then Aaron will not pass. The proctor will see Aaron cheat (if he does cheat) unless he (the Proctor) is blind. If the administration is not lax, then certainly the proctor is not blind. The administration is not lax. So if Aaron does not lie, he will not pass and will not cheat. (P,L,C,O,B,X)

44. If Smith is intelligent and studies hard, then he will get good grades and pass his courses. If Smith studies hard but lacks intelligence, then his efforts will be appreciated; and if his efforts are appreciated, he will pass his courses. If Smith is intelligent, then he does study hard. So, Smith will pass his courses. (I,S,G,P,E)

45. If you make an A in Logic, then Dean Bennett will give you a hug and the Controller will give you a $1000 rebate on your tuition. Getting a hug from Dean Bennett or $1000 back on your tuition from the Controller clearly implies that you have a remarkable future ahead. If you do have a remarkable future ahead, then you will eventually become a member of the power elite. So if you make an A in logic, you will eventually become a member of the power elite. (A,B,C,F,M)

46. You can take either History 101 (World History) for credit or History 111 (European History) for credit, but not both. So, you can take

History 101 for credit if and only if you do not take History 111 for credit. (W,E)

47. If you cheat then you will get nailed. If you cheat, then if you get nailed, then you will be expelled. If cheating is sufficient to get you expelled, then the rules must be very strict. The rules are very strict if and only if the Dean is really hard-nosed. It follows that the Dean is really hard-nosed. (C,N,E,R,H)

48. I will make an A in Logic and a B in Economics only if I settle for a C in History. If I settle for a C in History or get a D in Biology, then I will catch flack from my Father unless I lie about how easy my courses are. So, if I don't lie about how easy my courses are and make an A in Logic, then I will catch flack from my Dad. (A,B,C,D,F,L)

49. Eastern Airlines' current management will be victorious unless the end of Eastern's current strike occurs when and only when Bush nationalizes the air transportation system. Lorenzo will complete the shuttle deal with Trump if and only if Eastern Airlines' current management is not victorious. If the completion of this deal, along with the end of Eastern's current strike, is enough to cause Bush to nationalize the air transportation system, then the Carter/Reagan deregulation program is a dead letter. So that program is down the tubes. (V,E,N,L,D)

50. If Bill watches his diet and exercises he'll be fit. Watching his diet will make him lose weight and be ill tempered. So, if he both exercises and watches his diet, he will be both fit and ill tempered. (D,E,F,L,I)

51. If you eat raw rutabagas, you have strong teeth and a clear complexion. If you eat raw garlic, you have strong breath and few friends. If you have strong teeth and strong breath, then your dentist will rarely want to see you. So, if you eat raw rutabagas and raw garlic, your dentist will rarely want to see you. (R,T,C,G,B,F,D)

52. If Coca-Cola changes it formula then it will lose market share and RC Cola will have a chance to survive. But if Coke loses market share, neither Pepsi nor Dr. Pepper will be passive bystanders at the loss. Dr. Pepper will not be a passive bystander at Coke's loss if and only if its own marketing ambitions swell. So, if RC Cola is to have a chance to survive and Pepsi is not a passive bystander at Coke's loss, then Dr. Pepper's marketing ambitions will swell. (C,L,R,P,D,A)

53. If that is pasta then it is starchy; and if it is fattening then it is unhealthful. If it is pasta, then if it is starchy it is fattening. It is healthful

unless it is pasta and has no essential vitamins. So it is pasta if and only if it is fattening. (P,S,F,H,V)

54. Nimoy will become senile and Kelly will die unless Star Trek V is out before 1995. Star Trek V will not be out before then unless film distribution is reorganized and some copyright wrangles are settled. So, either Nimoy will become senile or Kelly will die; and either film distribution will be reorganized or some copyright wrangles will be settled. (N, K,S,F,C)

55. Either the tycoons will suppress the masses or the masses will exterminate the tycoons. If the failure of the tycoons to suppress the masses means that they will be exterminated by the masses, then the global political system is rotten. But the global political system is rotten and Marx is correct about the future, if and only if there is going to be general class warfare. Now, either capitalism is doomed or else the tycoons will suppress the masses and there will be no general class warfare. So, If Marx is correct about the future, then capitalism is doomed. (S,E,G,M,W,C)

56. If Bill is hungry, then if he eats fast he will have a belly-ache. He will eat fast if he is hungry. If it is true that his being hungry will result in his having a belly-ache, then Bill ought to change his eating habits. Bill is going to have a belly-ache unless his digestive system is O.K. So, if his digestive system is O.K., Bill need not change his eating habits. (H,F,B, C,D)

57. If I eat pears I'll ingest Alar and if I eat grapes I'll ingest cyanide. I won't get enough vitamins unless I eat either pears or grapes. So I will get enough vitamins only if I ingest either Alar or Cyanide. (P,A,G,C,V)

58. If you eat at either McDonald's or Hardee's, you will have a burger and fries. If you have either a burger or fries, your meal will be high in sodium and cholesterol. So, if you eat at Hardee's your meal will be high in cholesterol. (M,H,B,F,S,C)

59. If the Reds are the visiting team, the Braves will win. If the Hawks are the visiting team, the Braves will win. If the Braves win, I will clean up on the office pool. So, if I do not clean up on that pool then neither the Reds nor the Hawks are the visiting team. (R,B,H,C)

60. If John goes aardvark hunting, his vacation will not be boring; and if he goes white water canoeing, it will be dangerous. He will do one or the other; and it is just false that his vacation will be boring if and only if it is not dangerous. Consequently, it will be dangerous but not boring. (A,B,C,D)

61. I will take a vacation only if I go to Europe, and I will take one. If I go to Europe then I will certainly tour Scandinavia; and if I do that, then I'll cruise a fjord and be bored. But if I vacation and go to Europe, then I will certainly not be bored. It follows that I'll take a vacation if and only if I stay out of Scandinavia. (V,E,S,F,B)

62. If the leaves fall I will rake them. If the leaves fall, then if I rake them then I will be exhausted. If the falling of the leaves implies my exhaustion, then I am in poor condition. I am neither in poor condition nor lazy. Therefore, I will hire a yard-man. (F,R,E,P,L,Y)

63. If the prince returns then the queen will be happy and the royal throne will be secure. If our ships increase trade or if the queen is happy, then taxes will decrease. So, if the prince returns, then taxes will decrease. (P,Q,R,S,T)

64. It isn't April unless the dogwood is in bloom and the pollen count is sky-high. Crepe myrtle blooms if and only if the summer solstice has passed. Dogwood and crepe myrtle don't bloom at the same time. So, if the summer solstice is past, then it isn't April. (A,D,P,C,S)

65. I will plant pansies unless the soil is hard and the thrips are out of control. The claim that the soil is hard unless May rains have started is false. If May rains have not yet started, then the azaleas are still blooming. So I will plant pansies if and only if the azaleas are still blooming. (P,S,T,M,A)

66. There will be a gas shortage unless both oil exploration and industry efficiency increase. If OPEC has its own way, then there will be oil price stability if and only if the PLO is recognized by Israel. If Israel recognizing the PLO will produce oil price stability, then if there is a recession in the US then there will be no gas shortage. Industry efficiency will increase only if the US government funds refining research. So if OPEC has its way, then if there is a recession in the US, the US government will fund refining research   (G,E,I,O,S,P,R,F)

67. Khadafi will retain power only if the Americans and the British are powerless to prevent it. If either the Israelis or the Americans are powerless to prevent that, then terrorism will increase. If Khadafi's retaining power implies that terrorism will increase, then there will be no peace in the Middle East. So there will be no peace there. (K,A,B,I,T,P)

68. Charles will be King if and only if Elizabeth pre-deceases him or abdicates. The next monarch will be female only if Charles is never King.

If Charles lives to be 80, but never becomes King; and Elizabeth does not abdicate, but does pre-deceases him, then there must be a missing heir. So, if the next monarch is female, there is a missing heir. (K,P,A,F,L,H)

69. If today is Monday or Tuesday, this must be Paris. So if today is Tuesday, this must be Paris, Rome, Berlin or Athens. (M,T,P,R,B,A)

70. If good seed has been planted in the south 40, then the ground is fertile there only if plants are growing there. If Burpee's Big Boys are planted in the south 40, it will be good seed planted in fertile ground. Tom is an inept farmer unless Burpee's Big Boys are planted in the south 40. Either Andy or Tom is an inept farmer. Plants are not growing in the south 40. So unless Andy is an inept farmer, the ground in the south 40 is infertile. (G,F,P,B,T,A)

71. Either Belfast will become economically secure or the UK will shatter. But if England joins the EEC there will be a general recession, and if England does not join the EEC there will be a general strike. But the occurrence of either a general recession or a general strike will prevent Belfast from becoming economically secure. Therefore, unless Eire intervenes in Belfast, the UK will shatter. (B,U,J,R,S,E)

C: DIFFICULT PROBLEMS.

72. If you make 100% on either the final or the mid-term you will get an A in the course. So if you make 100% on both of them, you will surely get the A. (F, M, A)

73. On Monday I have French and on Tuesday I have History. Today is either Monday or Tuesday. If I have French or History then I must study. I must study if and only if there is to be a quiz today. So there will either be a quiz today or classes will be cancelled. (M,F,T,H,S,Q,C)

74. I will make an A on this exam only if I have beaten my brains out studying for it. I will win the departmental prize if and only if I make an A on this exam. I did not beat my brains out studying for this exam unless the textbook is viciously difficult. I will fail to win the departmental prize only if the textbook is viciously difficult. So it is a viciously difficult text. (A,B,W,T)

75 I am making an A on this exam; and I will get a B in the course unless my mid-term grade was hopeless. But, there will be no extra credit available for me unless I complete the main test with no serious mis-

takes. If I make an A on this exam and my mid-term grade was hopeless, then extra credit will be available for me. If I make no serious mistakes on the main test or if the grader is willing to overlook a few, then five solutions are necessary and sufficient for me to get a C overall. Therefore, if the claim that I have an A on the exam and a B in the course is false, then five solutions are necessary for me to get a C over-all. (A,B,H,X,M, S,W,F,C)

76.The make up exam is available if and only if you are sick and have a note from the Dean. You can have a note from the Dean only if you are sick or if there is a death in the family. So if there has been no death in the family and you missed the final exam and do have a note from the Dean, you have been sick and the make up exam is available. (M,S,N,D,F)

77. If it's Monday I have logic, and if it's Tuesday I have biology. It is either Sunday or Monday or Tuesday. So if it is not Sunday, then if I don't have logic I do have biology. (M,L,T,B,S)

78. Arnold can pass only if he reviews his notes, and Barbara can pass only if she works harder than usual. But if David can pass, then surely either Arnold or Barbara can. So, if Dave can pass, then if Barbara does not work harder than usual, Arnold will review his notes and can pass.(A,R, B,W,D)

79. If Beirut falls, then Syria is unbeatable. General Aoun and Col. Khadafi are both powerful leaders. Russia is still supplying tanks and planes to Libya if Khadafi is a powerful leader. There is hope for a middle-east truce if and only if Beirut does not fall. So either there is no hope at all for a middle-east truce (if Russia is still supplying tanks and planes to Libya), or else Syria can be beaten. (B,S,A,K,R,H)

80. If the demonstration is ready, then either the switch is already on, or else the technician's finger is on the button. If either the switch is already on or has been bypassed, then the demonstration is ready. So, if the technicians's finger is not on the button, then the demonstration is ready if and only if the switch is already on. (R,S,T,B)

81. I will quit if and only if I cannot solve this problem. If I am prepared, then I'll either solve this problem or know the reason why I can't solve it. Therefore, I am prepared only if my quitting implies that I know the reason why I can't solve this problem. (Q,S,P,K)

82. If you take logic you will be enlightened. If you take religion you will be blessed. You are not blessed unless your conduct improves; and

you are not enlightened without thinking more clearly. So, if you take logic or religion, either your conduct or thinking will take a turn for the better. (L,E,R,B,C,T)

83. Logic is fun. Hence, P is equivalent to Q if and only if it is the case that if either P or Q is true, then both P and Q are true. (L,P,Q)

84. Students of logic are militarily useful. For, if that were not the case, the Army would not want me. After all, I will not pass logic unless I study hard, and if I study hard the Army will want me. And, if I don't pass logic then I will lose my draft exemption and the Army will want me for sure. (M,A,P,S)

85. If you have the right algorithm your program won't crash. If your program doesn't crash and there is no power failure, you should have your solution by noon. If there is no power outage and you have your solution by noon, then you will get a high mark in LISP 101. If you do well in LISP 101, you should have no trouble in finding a good job when you graduate. So, if you have the right algorithm, then if you have your solution by noon you should have no trouble in finding a good job when you graduate. (A,C,F,S,M,J)

86. If Lola's History term paper was not on the assigned topic then she will fail History unless she exercises undue influence over her History professor. Lola's GPA will be 3.0 or better this term only if she does not fail history. If Lola is consistent, then her GPA will be 3.0 or better this term but her history term paper will not be on the assigned topic. Therefore if Lola is consistent, then she does exercise undue influence over her History professor. (T,F,I,G,C)

87. Brute can pass English only if he intimidates his English professor. Brute cannot intimidate his English professor unless that professor is a wimp. Brute's English professor is a wimp if and only if he prefers Keats to Hemingway. But, Brute will either pass English or Religion. If Brute passes religion, then either the religion department has no standards at all or Brute cheats in their course. The religion department does have some standards. So either Brute's English professor prefers Keats to Hemingway or Brute cheats in Religion. (E,I,W,P,R,S,C)

88. I must have the ability to program in COBOL if I make an B in this course; but the capacity to program in FORTRAN as well as COBOL would earn an A in it. My major will survive if and only if I make either an A or a B in this course. If my inability to program in COBOL implies that my major is down the tubes, then I've picked the wrong major. It

follows, consequently, that if I don't earn an A in this course, I have indeed picked the wrong major. (C,B,F,A,M,P)

89. The Honor System will not work unless students believe in it and professors care about it. Professors care about that system unless they are grossly underpaid, if and only if Economic Determinism is true. If Economic Determinism is true and incentives are low, then cultural malaise sets in. But this does not set in unless national priorities are all fouled up. So the Honor System does not work unless low incentives imply that national priorities are all fouled up. (H,S,P,G,E,I,M,N)

90. Logic is difficult unless one has a disciplined mind and a superb teacher. If logic is difficult unless one has a disciplined mind, then it is too hard for sophomores. Logic is neither too hard for sophomores nor impossible for freshmen, if the average student gets a C in it. The average student gets a C in logic if and only if the Gods are kind. The world is sometimes cruel, but either the Gods are kind or good luck is very common. Unfortunately, good luck is not very common. Therefore logic should be a required course for everyone. (D,M,T,S,F,C,K,W,L,R)

91. Ford will become the #1 automotive company in the U.S. if and only if GM loses market share. If Mazda builds engines for Ford, then if Wankel rotaries disappear, stratified carburetion will become the leader in internal combustion design. If advertising controls the marketplace, then GM will never lose market share. If Mazda builds engines for Ford, then Wankel rotaries will disappear. If Mazda's building engines for Ford entails that stratified carburetion becomes the leader in internal combustion design, then Ford will become the #1 automotive company in the U.S. So it follows that if advertising controls the marketplace, then the sale of automobiles has nothing to do with the quality of the product. (F,G,M,W, S,A,Q)

92. General Motors will stop making roller bearings if and only if both Hyatt and Timken increase their market share. Timken will achieve such an increase if and only if it sells bearings below cost. Timken will sell bearings below cost if it is foolishly optimistic about dominating the market. So, if Timken is foolishly optimistic about dominating the market and Hyatt increases its market share, General Motors will stop making roller bearings. (G,H,T,S,O)

93. I can avoid doing distributions if I use conditional proofs, and I can avoid universal generalizations if I use reductio proofs. I will use either conditional or reductio proofs, or limit myself to straight rules. Therefore, if I do go beyond straight rules, then if I don't avoid universal

generalizations I will avoid doing distributions. (D,C,U,R,L)

94. If I buy bonds, inflation will destroy my cash flow; and if I buy stocks, the recession will wipe out my equity. I will either buy mortgage notes, stocks, or bonds. So, if I don't buy mortgage notes, then if my cash flow is not destroyed by inflation my equity will be wiped out by the recession. (B,D,S,W,M)

95. Smith will mortgage her house and buy stocks on margin right now if she believes that the recent crash was only a technical adjustment; and if she does buy stocks on margin right now she will lose all her savings. If her broker is very clever, Smith does believe that the recent crash was only a technical adjustment. But if Smith loses all her savings, she will deprive her children of their inheritance. If Smith is not prudent and deprives her children of their inheritance, then she is a reprobate; and if she is a reprobate her children will wind up on welfare. So, if Smith's broker is very clever, then if Smith is not prudent her children will wind up on welfare. (M,S,B,L,C,I,P,R,W)

96. I cannot afford a Ferrari unless I have at least $100,000 in ready cash. I do not have that much ready cash. If I cannot afford a Ferrari, then I will not buy one. I will buy a Ferrari, a Honda Prelude or a Jeep. If I buy a Jeep, my wife will have to be satisfied with a stick shift. So, if she's not satisfied with a stick shift, then I will buy a Honda Prelude. (A,R,F,H, J,S)

97. We will run out of oil if and only if OPEC so chooses. If OPEC makes that choice, then when we do run out of oil steam cars will get another chance. If OPEC choosing for us to run out of oil means that steam cars will get another chance, then either Willys or Stanley Steamers will be back in business. South Bend will have a recession only if Willys does not get back into business. So, if OPEC chooses for us to run out of oil and South Bend has a recession, then Stanley Steamers will be back in business. (R,O,C,W,SS, SB)

98. Money is tight and blue-chip options are rare; but points will decline if and only if the RFB acts. If bonds decline, then stocks will rise; and if assessments do not hold steady, then bonds will decline. Stocks will rise unless blue chip options are rare; and I will refrain from quitting the market only if stocks rise. But stocks will rise if and only if money is tight; and either points or bonds will decline. So, I will quit the market unless points decline. (T,O,P,R,B,S,A,Q)

99. If inflation continues real earnings will decline; and if "bracket-creep" continues real taxes will climb. But, if real earnings decline and

real taxes climb, a taxpayer revolt is inevitable. "Bracket-creep" will continue unless there is a totally new tax law; and there will be a totally new tax law if and only if the first principle of supply-side economics is both true and false. So, if inflation continues, then a taxpayer revolt will occur if and only if taxes climb. (I,E,B,T,R,N,F)

100. We can get oil rights in either Aden or Burma only if Carter acts quickly. Carter will not act quickly unless Denmark and England sign the general treaty. Denmark will sign the general treaty only if England's signing it implies that France will sign it. Neither France nor Germany will sign it. We can get trading rights in Honduras if and only if we waive all import restrictions world-wide. If Germany does not sign the general treaty, then Japan will try to flood the US with steel and TV sets and we will not waive all import restrictions world-wide. We will either get oil rights in Burma or trading rights in Honduras or send Jimmy back to Klan Country. Our position of international leadership is secure unless we fail to send Jimmy back to Klan Country and continue to mess up in the Middle East. Therefore, our position of international leadership is secure. (A,B,C,D,E,F,G,H,I,J,K,L,M)

101. A refund is available if and only if your iron is broken and you can file form 102. You can file form 102 only if your iron is broken or was delivered defective. So, if your iron was not delivered defective but is not working, and if you can file form 102, then your iron is broken and you can get a refund. (R,B,F,D,W)

102. China will either occupy Taiwan or reach detente with Nong Won Kim. If Defense Department intelligence is correct, then China cannot both occupy Taiwan and improve the quality of its domestic life. China will reach detente with Nong Won Kim only if they make a long term loan or supply military aid to him. China will improve the quality of its domestic life unless the Defense Department's intelligence is incorrect. If China makes a long term loan to Nong Won Kim, the U.S. will not be upset. Far Eastern conflict will expand if China sends military aid to Nong Won Kim. If it is true that the U.S. will be upset if and only if Far Eastern conflict expands, then the Selective Service System will be reactivated. So, if Defense Department intelligence is correct, then if an expansion of conflict in the Far East will upset the U.S., then the Selective Service System will be reactivated. (T,N,D,Q,L,M,U,F,S)

103. If Bernie raises his prices or changes his sausage recipe, Tubby's will get more business. If either Tubby's or the Pizza Inn gets more business, then Bernie will try promotional gimmicks. If Bernie tries promotional gimmicks or gets a wine license, then competition will intensify on

the west end. If that competition intensifies or if a new cafe opens nearby, then even though some discounting will occur, Bernie will still raise his prices. So Bernie will raise his prices if and only if he tries promotional gimmicks. (R,C,T,P,G,W,I,N,D)

104. I will either buy or I will lease and pay interest. If my credit is good, I will not buy. I will lease and pay interest only if the interest charges are not taxable. Therefore, if my credit is good then the statement is false that I buy when and only when interest charges are not taxable. (B,L,I,G,T)

105. Windsor is an artificial name adopted in 1917. If that is true and Saxe-Coberg Gotha is the proper name of the royal family, then the Austrian line has not died out. Therefore the Austrian line has not died out if and only if the Austrian line has not died out. (W,S,A)

106. If there is no market crash, there will be national affluence. But if securities decline any further there will be a market crash. On the other hand, if securities do not decline further, then there will be neither a market crash nor national affluence. This shows that either (a) the occurrence of national affluence will cause securities to decline further if and only if there is a market crash, or (b) that Quayle will become president. (C,A, S,Q)

107. If the dollar plummets, the mark and the yen will skyrocket. If the yen skyrockets, Japan will go into hyperinflation unless the World Bank intervenes in the world economy to manipulate exchange rates. If U.S. tariffs are raised, neither the World Bank nor the IMF will intervene in the world economy to manipulate exchange rates. Therefore, if the dollar plummets and U.S. tariffs are increased, Japan will go into hyperinflation. (D,M,Y,J,W,T,I)

108. If Philip Morris buys Kraft, then a Virginia company will own both Lender's bagels and Sealtest ice cream as well as Miller beer and Yuban coffee. If RJR buys Nabisco, then a North Carolina company will own Oreo cookies as well as Birds Eye frozen foods. A Virginia company will own Lender's bagels and a North Carolina company will own Birds Eye frozen foods only if the industrial northeast is in economic ruin. The industrial northeast is not in economic ruin even though RJR has already bought Nabisco. So Philip Morris will not succeed in buying Kraft. (P,L, S,M,Y,R,O,B,E)

109. The unemployment rate will plunge if and only if inflation accelerates. If taxes are not increased, then the money supply will grow. If

productivity declines, demand for goods will increase. If the money supply grows, then if demand for goods increases, inflation will accelerate. If Bush keeps his word and Labor stages an industrial slowdown, then taxes will not be increased and productivity will decline (unless the unemployment rate plunges). However, Bush will keep his word about taxes and Labor will stage an industrial slow down unless the Golden Rule becomes the governing principle of the U.S. economy. But, neither the Golden Rule nor Total Altruism will ever become the governing principle of the U.S. economy. It follows, then, that inflation will accelerate.(U,I,T,M,P, D,B,L,G,A)

110. If azaleas will grow here, then marigolds and nasturtiums will too. If both marigolds and daisies will grow here, either heather or portulaca will grow here as well. If heather or gorse will grow here, columbines will too. Portulaca will grow here only if columbines will. So, if azaleas will grow here, then if daisies will then so will columbines. (A,M,N,D,H,P,G,C)

111. If Thatcher imposes a budget there will be no growth in British imports; and if the Royal allowance is cut there will be general outcry among the Tories. There can be monetary restraint if and only if Sterling is stabilized. If there is monetary restraint and Sterling is stabilized, then Thatcher will impose a budget or the Royal allowance will be cut. So, if there is either monetary restraint or if Sterling is stabilized, then there will be no growth in British imports or there will be general outcry among the Tories. (B,G,R,O,M,S)

112. The hostages will be released only if the militants grow more reasonable. The militants will grow more reasonable only if the U.S. is not perceived as supplying hardware to Israel. The U.S. will not be perceived as supplying hardware to Israel if and only if the U.S. is not supplying it to them and Russia restrains her propaganda war. So, if the hostages are released, the militants will have grown more reasonable and Russia will have held her propaganda war in check. (H,M,P,S,R)

113. I will visit the Canal Zone this Summer unless the American occupation of Panama lasts past June and Cuba continues to make trouble in the Caribbean. Grenada is a U.S. puppet; and Belize will support American intervention unless the U.K. condemns it. If it is true that I'll visit the Canal Zone this Summer unless the American occupation of Panama lasts past June, then I cannot finalize my vacation plans until Spring. But, if Grenada is a U.S. puppet and Belize supports American intervention, then I don't need to wait until Spring to finalize my vacation

plans. The U.K. will not condemn American intervention. It follows that I shall vacation in Venezuela this year. (Z,P,C,G,B,U,F,V)

114. If the money from North Sea oil comes to Westminster, then Britain will be solvent. If the money from North Sea oil comes to Westminster and Britain is solvent, then U.K. taxes will decline. If the money from North Sea oil comes to Westminster, then if U.K. taxes decline, the Scottish independence movement will collapse. If the Scottish independence movement collapses, then either U.K. taxes will decline or the money from North Sea oil will come to Westminster. It is simply false that either U.K. taxes will decline or that the Scottish independence movement will collapse. Therefore, the money from North Sea oil will come to Westminster if and only if the Scottish independence movement collapses. (M,B,T,S)

115. If the Greeks or the Yugoslavs rebel, then the Cypriots and the Turks will be threatened. If the Yugoslavs rebelling would cause the Turks to be threatened, then the Middle East is shaky. But the Middle East is shaky if and only if there is a chance of foreign intervention; and foreign intervention is impossible. So Bush's grand plan will work. (G,Y, C,T,M,F,P)

116. Russia will invade Poland unless the U.S. resists and world opinion solidifies. To say that the U.S. will resist unless the New York Times urges appeasement is just a lie. If the New York Times does not urge appeasement, then the Times Dispatch will. So, Russia will invade Poland if and only if the Times Dispatch urges appeasement. (R,U,W,N,T)

117. If either the Russian military high command or the Supreme Soviet believes that a nuclear war can be won, then a surprise attack will occur unless the U.S. sues for peace. If Americans keep their nerve, then the U.S. will not sue for peace. There will be a crisis in Moscow if an SDI treaty is signed or if Peking intervenes. Therefore, if the Supreme Soviet believes a nuclear war can be won and there is no crisis in Moscow, then if Americans keep their nerve, there will be a surprise attack and Peking will maintain a hands-off posture. (R,S,A,U,N,C,T,P)

118. If the Huns or the Goths are coming, then either the fort will be razed, the villages will be sacked, or the people will be killed. If Wotan is the High God, then neither will the temple be desecrated nor the villages sacked. Norse culture will survive if and only if the people are not killed. If Thor is powerful, then the invasion will be repelled and Norse culture will survive. Therefore, it is not the case that both Wotan is the High God and the Goths are coming, unless Thor's being powerful implies that while

the fort will be razed, the villages will not be sacked and the people will not be killed. (H,G,R,S,K,W,D,N,T,I)

119. If existentialism is irrational and Marxism is unscientific, then there is no good reason for subscribing to either the former or the latter view (if one wants to hold justified beliefs). If one isn't just silly, then one does want to hold justified beliefs (if one thinks that the world is coherent at all); and if one does not think that the world is coherent at all, then one is some kind of absurdist. So, if one thinks that the world is coherent at all, then if one isn't just silly, then there is no good reason for subscribing to Marxism (if, indeed, Marxism is unscientific and existentialism is irrational, as alleged). (E,M,F,L,J,S,C,A)

120. If Kennedy stays north of the Potomac, the Democrats have a chance at the Governor's position; and the Republicans have a chance at that position only if Bush is an effective president. If it is true that the Democrats have a chance at the Governor's position unless Bush is an effective president, then it follows that the Moral Majority will be blocked in Virginia only if Billy Graham denounces Jerry Falwell. The Republicans will have a chance at the Governor's position, and sweep the legislature, unless Kennedy stays north of the Potomac. If either Kennedy stays north of the Potomac or the Republicans sweep the legislature, then either the liberals will be unrepresented there or a new progressive coalition will be formed in the South. Therefore, if the Moral Majority is blocked in Virginia or the liberals are represented in the legislature, then either Graham will denounce Falwell or a new progressive coalition will be formed in the South (K,D,R,E,M,G,S,L,C)

THREE: PREDICATE PROBLEMS

A: EASY PROBLEMS.

1. Anyone will pass unless they have not studied. Margie has studied, so she will pass. (Px,Sx,m)

2. Athenian and Spartan are Greek dialects. All Greek dialects are Sanskrit derived. Therefore Athenian is Sanskrit derived. (a,s,Gx,Dx)

3. All professionals are educated. No administrators are illiterates. No illiterates are educated. So some administrators are professionals. (Px,Ex,Ax,Ix)

4. Everyone is a liberal, a conservative or an anarchist. If one is a conservative but not reactionary, then one supports free trade and low taxes. So one can support low taxes and not be an anarchist only if one is not a liberal. (Lx,Cx,Ax,Rx,Fx,Tx)

5. Every Communist is tricky. Nobody who is tricky should be allowed to teach the young. Only those who read the Daily Worker are Communists. Some U.R. faculty members read the Daily Worker. So some U.R. faculty members should not be allowed to teach the young. (Cx,Tx,Ax,Rx,Fx)

6. All periwinkles are blue all over. Nothing is both blue all over and red all over. So nothing that is red all over is a periwinkle. (Px,Bx,Rx)

7. All Republicans are conservative. Some professors are Republicans. Some conservatives are wealthy. Therefore, some professors are wealthy. (Rx,Cx,Px,Wx)

8. A properly edited campus literary magazine will make a positive contribution to campus intellectual life. *The Messenger* is a campus literary magazine. So, if it is properly edited, it contributes positively to the intellectual life of the college. (Lx,Ex,Cx,m)

9. Logic is a snap. If logic is a snap, Brute will graduate. Anyone who graduates will get a job. Therefore someone will graduate and get a job. (Sx,l,Gx,b,Jx)

10. Marzipan and nougat are edible only when fresh. Therefore all fresh nougat is edible. (Mx,Nx,Ex,Fx)

11. Betas and Fijis party non-stop. Anyone who parties non-stop is going to die young. Clyde is a Fiji. It follows that Clyde will die young. (Bx,Fx,Px,Dx,c)

12. The Ku Klux Klan accepts Christians but not Jews. Christians and Jews are both accepted by the Lions Club. A group that bars Jews or Christians is bigoted. No group accepting both Jews and Christians is bigoted. Therefore, the KKK is bigoted and the Lions Club is not. (Cx,Jx, Bx,k,l)

13. No angel is mortal. All Greeks are humans. Every human dies. Socrates was a Greek. So Socrates was not an angel. (Ax,Mx,Gx,Hx,s)

14. All Naturopaths are quacks. Some Virginians are Naturopaths. Some quacks are fanatics. So, some Virginians are fanatics. (Nx,Qx,Vx, Fx)

15. A first-rate Christmas tree is either a Scotch Pine or a blue spruce. A Christmas tree that is Georgia-grown can't be a blue spruce. My Christmas tree is a first-rate Christmas tree, and it was grown in Georgia. So my Christmas tree is a Scotch Pine. (Fx,Cx,Sx,Bx,Gx,m)

16. Everything is either material or spiritual. Something is both green and round. Only things that can be located in space and time are material. Nothing that is round is spiritual. So there exists at least one material thing that can be located in space and time. (Mx,Sx,Gx,Rx,Lx)

17. No spotted animals are striped animals. Some spotted animals are dogs. Some striped animals are cats. So no dogs are cats. (Ax,SPx,STx, Dx,Cx)

18. All monkeys have prehensile tails. While some monkeys are herbivores, all monkeys are mortal. Not all mortal things have prehensile tails, however. So there is at least one mortal thing that is not a herbivore. (Mx,Px,Hx,Dx)

19. Some fish are smooth-skinned. Some fish are green. Anything

that is both green and smooth-skinned is an evolutionary anomaly. Therefore some fish are evolutionary anomalies. (Fx,Sx,Gx,Ex)

20. Everything is either impossible or disappointing. No climb to the top of Mt. Everest is impossible. A genuine contribution to human happiness and well being is never disappointing. Therefore, no climb to the top of Mt. Everest is a genuine contribution to human happiness and well being. (Ix,Dx,Cx,Gx,)

21. Only intelligent people are college graduates. Some politicians are demagogues. No demagogues are intelligent people. So some politicians are not college graduates. (Ix,Cx,Px,Dx)

22. The bird I am looking at is either a grosbeak or a finch. No finch has a white bill. The bird I am looking at has a red rump, yellow coverts, white bill and black wings. All grosbeaks and tanagers are native to Canada. Things that are native to Canada are incidentals in Virginia. Therefore the bird I am looking at must be incidental in Virginia. (b,Gx, Fx,Wx,Rx,Yx,Bx,Tx,Nx,Ix)

23. All puppies are warm and huggy. All puppies are delightful if they are warm and huggy. Some puppies are not delightful. Therefore, kittens and lambs are cute. (Px,Wx,Hx,Dx,Kx,Lx,Cx)

B: TRANSITIONAL PROBLEMS. (Easy with Conditional Proof techniques, but Medium without).

24. Whiskey and gin are foul-tasting depressants. So gin is a depressant. (Wx,Gx,Fx,Dx)

25. Any Bugatti is fast. Therefore any Bugatti with Pirelli tires is a fast Bugatti. (Bx,Fx,Px)

26. Mercedes and Jaguars are expensive to buy. Being expensive to buy and being expensive to repair are each sufficient conditions for being beyond the reach of a philosophy professor. So a Jaguar is beyond the reach of a philosophy professor. (Mx,Jx,Bx,Rx,Px)

27. No perfect being is immoral. Any being that fails to value intellectual honesty is imperfect. No moral being which values intellectual honesty would punish agnosticism. So, if God is a perfect being, She will not punish agnosticism. (Px,Mx,Vx,Ax,g)

28. Mennonites and Quakers are religiously conservative and socially liberal. Anyone who is socially liberal and economically progressive is in favor of reverse taxation. Therefore, a Quaker who is economically progressive will favor either reverse taxation or wage subsidies. (Mx,Qx, Rx,Sx,Ex,Tx,Wx)

29. Apples, oranges, dates, and figs are good sources of vitamin C as well as being tasty and cheap. So figs are tasty. (Ax,Ox,Dx,Fx,Gx,Tx,Cx)

30. Snails are an exotic delicacy. Real Men don't eat exotic delicacies. Therefore a jumbo French snail, garlic-drenched and served with Tattinger '68, is not something that a Real Man would eat. (Sx,Dx,Ex, Jx,Fx,Gx,Tx)

31. Plums and grapes are juicy and tart. Nothing is tart unless it is acidic. Therefore plums are acidic. (Px,Gx,Jx,Tx,Ax)

32. LeBarons and Rivieras are ostentatious and expensive. Anything that is either expensive or hard to repair is both impractical and needless. So Rivieras are impractical. (Lx,Rx,Ox,Ex,Hx,Ix,Nx)

33. Communists and fascists are ideologues and political chauvinists. Every ideologue and every zealot is dangerous and untrustworthy. So, communists are untrustworthy. (Cx,Fx,Ix,Px,Zx,Dx,Tx)

34. Representatives and Senators are Congressmen. All Congressmen and Morticians are either altruistic or hypocritical. No Representative is altruistic. So, all Representatives are hypocrites. (Rx,Sx,Cx,Mx,Ax,Hx)

C: MEDIUM PROBLEMS.

35. All Methodists and Nazarenes are arminian and evangelistic. All arminians and all charismatics are neither Thomists nor predestinarians. Therefore no Nazarenes are predestinarians. (Mx,Nx,Ax,Ex,Cx,Tx,Px)

36. All of the nominees are Americans who speak French. Some American business people are true chauvinists. No truly chauvinistic Americans speak either French or Russian. So no American nominees are business people. (Nx,Ax,Fx,Bx,Cx,Rx)

37. American military leaders are either completely apolitical or are right wing. There is at least one individual who is not right wing but who

is a bigot. Therefore there is at least one individual who, if not a bigot, is either not an American military leader or not right wing. (Ax,Mx,Px,Rx, Bx)

38. Among academics, only blind ambition produces a temper for administration. So an academic with a temper for administration, marginal social concern and ruthless morals, will have blind ambition, egomania, megalomania or delusions of grandeur. (Ax,Bx,Tx,Sx,Rx,Ex,Mx,Dx)

39. Logic, accounting, calculus and macro-economics are demanding, precise and stimulating. So macro-economics is stimulating. (Lx,Ax,Cx, Mx,Dx,Px,Sx)

40. Every U.R. dean goes on to be a college president unless they die under thirty. No U.R. dean who dies under thirty goes on to be a college president. Therefore it is true of all U.R. deans that either a) they live to be thirty or older and go on to be a college president, or b) they die before thirty and do not go on to be a college president. (Rx,Dx,Px,Tx)

41. Everything can be spatially and temporally located unless it is unreal. Anything that can be located in time but not in space is either a mental abstraction or Divine. So everything both Divine and real can be located in time. (Sx,Tx,Rx,Mx,Dx)

42. No politician is honest. All non-politicians are naive. Anyone qualified to be President must be honest and not naive. So no one is qualified to be President. (Px,Hx,Nx,Qx)

43. Almost all who take logic pass it. Those who do take and pass logic are excellent candidates for the Law School. ZDK pledges all of the excellent Law School candidates, and it does not pledge anyone else. So there is at least one successful logic student who was pledged by ZDK. (Tx,Px,Cx,Zx)

44. All citizens who are not traitors are here at the meeting. Every government official is a citizen. There are some government officials who are not here at the meeting. So there is at least one traitor. (Cx,Tx, Mx,Gx)

45. Freshmen and Sophomores are undergraduates and naive. No undergraduate or person under eighteen has the AB degree or can vote. So Freshmen cannot vote. (Fx,Sx,Ux,Nx,Ex,Ax,Vx)

46. Anyone who scores above 90 on the mid-term and the final will get an A in Accounting. Anyone who mastered Chapter 6 will score above 90 on the mid-term. Anyone who mastered Chapter 8 will score above 90 on the final. Someone will make an A in Accounting. Consequently, someone must have mastered both Chapter 6 and Chapter 8. (Mx,Fx,Ax,Sx,Ex)

47. Only those who score above 90 on both the mid-term and the final will get an A in logic. Only those who mastered Chapter 6 will score above 90 on the mid-term; and only those who mastered Chapter 8 will score above 90 on the final. Someone will make an A in logic. So someone must have mastered both Chapters 6 and 8. (Mx,Fx,Ax,Sx,Ex)

48. Anything floats if and only if its specific gravity is less than that of its surrounding medium. Everything that floats is difficult to catch. All hydrogen bubbles are of less specific gravity than their surrounding medium. No hard to catch hydrogen bubbles are static. Therefore no hydrogen bubbles at all are static. (Fx,Gx,Dx,Hx,Sx)

49. Nobody who is less than completely honest deserves an office of public trust. Anyone who does not deserve an office of public trust should be barred from running for office. Some lawyers are highly intelligent. However, high intelligence does not guarantee complete honesty. Therefore, there are lawyers who should be barred from running for office. (Hx,Tx,Bx,Lx,Ix)

50. Some metal atoms will oxidize. Ever metal atom emits rays. Everything that has parts and emits rays can be split. Anything that will oxidize has parts. Therefore some metallic atoms can be split. (Mx,Ox, Rx,Px,Sx)

51. All travelers who visit Pago-Pago must fly Air Fiji. All American chauvinists ridicule third-world cultures. Anyone who ridicules third-world cultures and flies Air Fiji will get culture shock. So any American chauvinist traveler who visits Pago-Pago will get culture shock. (Tx,Px, Fx,Ax,Cx,Rx,Kx)

52. Everyone in the class who did their homework passed. Only naive sophomores would fail to do their homework. Some in the class were sophomores; but none in the class were naive. So everyone in the class passed. (Cx,Hx,Px,Nx,Sx)

53. Littlenecks and Cherrystones are mollusks. Any Delaware mol-

lusk is edible. Therefore any Delaware Littleneck is edible. (Lx,Cx,Mx, Dx, Ex)

54. Not all persons who reside in Richmond love the city. Among those persons who do reside in Richmond, only those who love it are strongly opposed to social change. No one who is strongly opposed to social change is of any interest to Teddy Kennedy, but everybody else is. So there is at least one person who resides in Richmond who is of interest to Teddy Kennedy. (Px,Rx,Lx,Ox,Ix)

55. Only business majors can use the SBA lounge. Frank is not a business major. Anyone who cannot use the SBA lounge is the target of unfair discrimination. One is the target of unfair discrimination if and only if their rights are being violated or carelessly over-ridden. Frank's rights are not being violated. Frank's rights are being carelessly over-ridden only if he is a passive and non-demanding person. It follows that Frank is a non-demanding person. (Bx,Ux,f,Tx,Vx,Ox,Px,Nx)

56. Snakes and lizards are reptiles. Reptiles and birds are oviparous. Therefore snakes are oviparous. (Sx,Lx,Rx,Bx,Ox)

57. Male and female humans all die. Socrates was a male human and Zantippe was a female human. It follows that neither one of them was immortal. (Mx,Fx,Hx,Dx,s,z)

58. No Lotus that is properly lubricated will throw a rod if it is well driven. Any Lotus prepared by Team Eavensham is properly lubricated. A properly lubricated Lotus that does not throw a rod will finish the race. Every Lotus that finishes the race is well driven. So, any Lotus prepared by Team Eavensham will finish the race if and only if it is well driven. (Lx,Px,Tx,Wx,Ex,Fx)

59. Some U.R. students are either Freshmen or Sophomores. Some U.R. students major in both philosophy and history. Any Freshman who majors in philosophy and history is a genius. Therefore at least one U.R. student is a genius. (Ux,Fx,Sx,Px,Hx,Gx)

60. Someone cheated on the logic midterm. Anyone who does that is loathsome and contemptible. Only a scoundrel is contemptible. Any loathsome contemptible scoundrel deserves expulsion. Anyone who cheated on the logic midterm must be enrolled in logic. It follows that someone who is enrolled in logic deserves to be expelled. (Mx,Lx,Cx,Sx,Dx,Ex)

61. One who marries for cash will never find affection; and one who marries for love will never find riches. Those who don't find affection and those who don't find riches live wretched lives. No one whose life is wretched or who has no self-esteem is a suitable role-model for the young. Any philosopher who marries at all marries for love. Therefore, no married philosopher is a suitable role-model for the young. (Cx,Ax, Lx,Rx,Wx,Ex,Sx,Px,Mx)

62. Snacks are good if and only if they are tasty. Anything that is tasty is either aromatic, crunchy, or nibbleable. If a thing is tasty and juicy, then it is not crunchy. There is at least one tasty and juicy snack that is not nibbleable. So there is at least one tasty and juicy snack that is aromatic. (Sx,Gx,Tx,Ax,Cx,Nx,Jx)

63. Cheap gin is raw and fierce-tasting. Nothing is fierce-tasting unless it is hard to digest. Anything that is hard to digest is unsuitable for a gourmet dinner. All and only unappetizing things are unsuitable for gourmet dinners. It follows that cheap gin is never appetizing. (Gx,Cx, Rx,Fx,Hx,Sx,Ax)

64. Barracudas and sharks are aggressive and vicious. Some fish are not vicious. No fish are cartilaginous except sharks. Sharks are fish. So some fish that are not cartilaginous are not sharks. (Bx,Sx,Ax,Vx,Fx,Cx)

65. No Alar-laced fruit is beneficial to your health. Some California peaches are beneficial to your health. All peaches are fruit. So, some California fruit is not Alar-laced. (Fx,Ax,Bx,Cx,Px)

66. Sun-dried annelida and *framboises du bois* are both exotic and costly. Subtly flavored items and exotic items are sought after by gourmets and dilettantes. Any item that is either sought after by gourmets or is "in" in California will be popular among Richmond Yuppies and available at the Butlery. So, sun-dried annelida must be available either at the Butlery or at *La Maisonette*. (Ax,Fx,Ex,Cx,Sx,Gx, Dx,Ix,Yx,Bx,Lx)

67. Cheaters either think they will never get caught or have some sort of death wish. Anyone who believes they are uncatchable is irrational. Nobody with any sort of death wish is emotionally stable. Only rational people pass logic. So no one who passes logic and is emotionally stable cheats. (Cx,Nx,Dx,Rx,Sx,Lx)

68. Some 18 year old football players are bright and articulate.

Richmond wants any football player who is a potential scholar. No one who is neither a potential scholar nor a scholar already is both bright and articulate. No 18 year olds are scholars already. Therefore there is at least one football player that Richmond wants. (Ex,Fx,Bx,Ax,Rx,Px,Sx)

69. All Hegelian propositions are relational, and all Aristotelian propositions are predicative. Some Aristotelian propositions are metaphysical. Some metaphysical propositions are obscure. All Hegelian propositions are obscure. So no Aristotelian propositions are relational. (Hx,Rx,Ax,Px,Mx,Ox)

70. Freshmen and Sophomores are underclassmen. Underclassmen and draft resisters are anti-establishment. So Freshmen are anti-establishment. (Fx,Sx,Ux,Dx,Ax)

D: HARD PROBLEMS.

71. Italy and Germany are nations that where enemies of the U.S. and were badly beaten in World War II. Any nation which was badly beaten in that war and is able to learn from history is consciously in favor of binding peace treaties. Therefore, if Germany is able to learn from history, it consciously favors either binding peace treaties or national suicide. (i,g, Nx,Ex,Bx,Ax,Tx,Sx)

72. No President who is a loyal Democrat is going to appoint Republicans. It is impossible to appoint a Nixon crony without appointing a Republican. Therefore a President who appoints Haldeman is not a loyal Democrat. That is because any President who appoints Haldeman is appointing a Nixon crony. (Px,Lx,Rx,Nx,Hx)

73. All Virginians who vote in national elections vote conservative. All fundamentalists pray frequently. Anyone who votes conservative and prays frequently favors public school prayers. So any fundamentalist Virginian who votes in national elections will vote conservative and favor public school prayers. (Vx,Nx,Cx,Fx,Px,Sx)

74. If one eats at Tubby's, one will have either a DeathBurger, salsa salad or a Pedro Patty. If one eats a DeathBurger, one gets cramps. Those who eat salsa salad become flatulent. If you eat a Pedro Patty, you die. Not everyone avoids eating at Tubby's. So somebody gets cramps, becomes flatulent or dies. (Tx,Bx,Sx,Px,Cx,Fx,Dx)

75. Everyone who teaches is a philosopher. Everyone is either a

teacher or a student. Some Greeks are not teachers. Anyone who is a student has much to learn. The claim that some philosophers have lots to learn is a false claim. So some Greeks who are not philosophers have much to learn. (Tx,Px,Sx,Gx,Lx)

76. A GM car is affordable if and only if it costs less than an average year's salary. Some affordable GM cars are Buicks and not Chevrolets. All GM cars that are Buicks are reliable. All GM cars are Chevrolets unless they cost over $8000. A GM car costs over $8000 and is reliable only if it has been individually test-driven at the company proving ground. It follows that some GM cars that cost less than an average year's salary are individually test-driven at the company proving ground. (Gx,Ax,Lx,Bx,Cx,Rx,Ox,Tx)

77. Every undergraduate is either a greek or an independent, but not both. Every greek is either in a fraternity or a sorority, but not both. Among greeks, only those in sororities support open rush and strict carding at rush parties. So an undergraduate who is not an independent will support open rush and strict carding only if not in a fraternity. (Ux,Gx, Ix,Fx,Sx,Ox,Cx)

78. No automobile is popular with the college crowd unless it is both fast and sexy-looking. Nothing is check rated by *Consumer Reports* unless it is both safe and reliable. Nothing fast is safe. Nothing reliable is sexy-looking. So a car that is both popular with the college crowd and check rated by *Consumer Reports* would have to be extremely expensive. (Ax,Px,Fx,Lx,Cx,Sx,Rx,Ex)

79. Franklin and Lazer computers all run Appleworks. No computer will run Appleworks without either Prodos or a Prodos knock-off for its operating system. Only computers authorized by Apple have Prodos for their operating system. Lazer computers are not authorized by Apple. Any computer with a Prodos knock-off for its operating system violates the spirit of the copyright law. Computers that violate the spirit of the copyright law do not sell at all well unless they are economically priced. Franklin and Lazer computers sell very well. So Lazer computers must be economically priced. (Cx,Fx,Lx,Rx,Px,Kx,Ax,Vx,Sx,Ex)

80. Biblical days began at sunset. Therefore the world will end tomorrow or it will not. (Bx,Sx,Wx,Ex)

81. Evangelists and faith healers all say they are morally pure. Jim Bakker, an evangelist, has been indicted for tax evasion and accused of

fornication. No one guilty of a felony is morally pure. Anyone convicted for tax evasion is guilty of a felony. Anyone who says that he is morally pure but is not morally pure is a liar. Those indicted and tried for tax evasion are always convicted of it. So Jim Bakker will be tried for tax evasion only if he is a liar. (Ex,Hx,Sx,b,Ix,Ax,Gx,Mx,Cx,Lx,Tx)

82. Saints and mystics are devout and other-worldly. Only the truly virtuous are devout. No one is truly virtuous without being godly and pure. One is pure if and only if one is a saint. So, if one is either a saint or devout, one is both a saint and devout. (Sx,Mx,Dx,Ox,Vx,Gx,Px)

83. Whatever is lightweight floats and whatever is organic generates heat. Therefore, if everything is either lightweight or organic, then everything either floats or generates heat. (Lx,Fx,Ox,Gx)

84. Krypton alone yields Z-rays. Krypton is capable of paralyzing Superman and helping crooks. Only all things that can harm humans can help criminals. That object there is krypton. Krypton is completely harmless to humans. So that object there is capable of paralyzing Captain Marvel. (Zx,Kx,Sx,Cx,Hx,t,Mx)

85. All except male athletes are eligible for the prize. Not all the athletes are ineligible. All athletes are either male or female. So there is at least one female athlete who is eligible. (Mx,Ax,Ex,Fx)

86. Every athlete at this college who is any good at all is nationally famous. And, as a matter of fact, no one who goes to this college and is neither a bookworm nor a weakling is a poor athlete. It should be pointed out, however, that no one attends this college who is not an athlete. And, of course, no athlete is a weakling. But, sad to say, there are individuals going to this college who are not nationally famous. We are forced to conclude that there is at least one bookworm at this college, consequently. (Ax,Cx,Gx,Fx,Bx,Wx)

87. All humans are practical and skeptical-minded. No one who is practical majors in philosophy. Some U.R. undergraduates are philosophy majors. Only intelligent beings go to college. One cannot be a U.R. undergraduate without going to college. All non-human intelligent beings are space aliens. Therefore there is at least one space alien that is a U.R. undergraduate. (Hx,Px,Sx,Mx,Ux,Ix,Cx,Ax)

88. A pure-bred dog is show quality if and only if its appearance is flawless. Some show quality pure-bred dogs are short-legged and have no

tail.   Any short legged pure-bred dog is likely to sit down during show trials.   Every pure-bred dog has a tail unless it has been removed.   A pure-bred dog that has had its tail removed and is likely to sit down during show trials will get a cold rump during winter dog shows.   Therefore some pure-bred dogs who have flawless appearance will get a cold rump during winter dog shows.   (Qx,Ax,Lx,Tx,Sx,Rx,Cx)

89. Some grosbeaks are seen in Virginia; but no grosbeaks are seen in Tennessee.   Grosbeaks and finches are small birds.   Any bird seen in Virginia but not in Tennessee is either coastal or migratory.   Neither owls nor grosbeaks are coastal.   So some grosbeaks must be migratory.   (Gx, Vx,Tx,Fx,Sx,Bx,Cx,Mx,Ox)

90. Anything that steals is a thief.   Anything that snatches is greedy. Squirrels steal, snatch and sneak.   A greedy thief that sneaks does not deserve to live.   The law does not allow killing squirrels.   Anything that does not deserve to live but cannot be lawfully killed makes a mockery of the law.   It follows that squirrels make a mockery of the law.   (STx,Tx, SNx,Gx,SQx,SKx,Dx,Kx,Mx)

91. A fruit is a drupe if and only if it is an apple or a pear.   No berries are drupes.   So no fruit is both a pear and a berry.   (Fx,Dx,Ax,Px,Bx)

92. Apples, oranges and grapes are delicious, nutritious and healthful. Nutritious things and flavorful things are both valuable and marketable. If oranges are marketable then, if they are expensive to buy, they are lucrative to raise.   Oranges are perishable.   It follows that oranges are perishable if and only if they are lucrative to raise if expensive to buy.   (Ax, Ox,Gx,Dx,Nx,Hx,Fx,Vx,Mx,Ex,Lx,Px)

93. All who study logic will be wise.   All who study economics or business administration will be powerful.   If anyone studies religion, they will be holy. Therefore anyone who is neither powerful, holy nor wise, must not have studied logic, religion or economics.   (Lx,Wx,Ex,Bx,Px,Rx, Hx)

94. It is simply false that all philosophers are worth studying. Nevertheless, it is true of philosophers that all of the bright ones are informative.   It is also true that every logician is a bright philosopher. Furthermore, every informative person is worth studying.   So there is at least one philosopher who is not a logician. (Px,Wx,Bx,Ix,Lx)

95. All Freshmen and Sophomores are naive and innocent.   No atheists

are either naive or innocent. Some undergraduates at Westhampton are atheists. Every undergraduate is either a Freshman, Sophomore, Junior or Senior. Anyone who is not naive is a cynic. Therefore at least one Westhampton Junior or Senior is a cynic. (Fx,Sx,Nx,Ix,Ax,Ux,Wx,Jx, SRx,Cx)

96. Any agreeable person has either genuine empathy for others or a charming personality. No inadequately socialized person has genuine empathy for others. But a person who is adequately socialized does have both a charming personality and delightful manners. Anyone who has a charming personality or who is humorous, is good company unless they are insincere. Anyone who is good company is both agreeable and tactful. So, among sincere people, one is agreeable if and only if one has a charming personality. (Ax,Ex,Cx,Ix,Mx,Hx,Gx,Sx,Tx)

97. All thorny plants are difficult to harvest. Some thorny plants yield major profits at harvest time. So the claim that nothing difficult to harvest yields a major profit at harvest time is false. (Tx,Dx,Yx)

98. Only all furze is gorse. If all furze is gorse, then no furze is edible. If only furze is gorse, then all gorse is picturesque. There is such a thing as furze. So, something inedible is picturesque. (Fx,Gx,Ex,Px)

99. Some mammals are tame. All mammals have hair and are warm-blooded. All small, tame mammals are cuddly. Anything cuddly is lovable. Dogs are mammals. No Alsatian dogs are small; but not all dogs are Alsatians. It follows that any hairless dog that is not an Alsatian is lovable. (Mx,Tx,Hx,Wx,Sx,Cx,Lx,Dx,Ax)

100. One can take the senior seminar without getting individual permission if and only if one is a philosophy major. No one who is taking baby logic in their senior year is a philosophy major. Only those who can take the senior seminar without individual permission are eligible to attempt the $5000 prize problem. But if no one who is taking baby logic in their senior year is eligible to attempt the $5000 prize problem, then the philosophy department has too many rules. Therefore, if the philosophy department does not have too many rules, then anyone can take the senior seminar without getting individual permission. (Tx,Mx,Bx,Ex,p,Rx)

FOUR: SENTENTIAL SOLUTIONS

1. **1. P ≡ W**
    2. (W ⊃ P) ⊃ ~H   /∴   ~H
    3. (P ⊃ W) · (W ⊃ P)   1   MEA
    4. (W ⊃ P) · (P ⊃ W)   3   Com
    5. W ⊃ P   4   Simp
    6. ~H   2,5   MP

2. **1. H ≡ ~W**
    2. ~W   /∴   **H ∨ C**
    3. (H ⊃ ~W) · (~W ⊃ H)   1   MEA
    4. (~W ⊃ H) · (H ⊃ ~W)   3   Com
    5. ~W ⊃ H   4   Simp
    6. H   5,2   MP
    7. H ∨ C   6   Add

3. **1. I ∨ M**
    2. M ⊃ T
    3. ~I · (T ⊃ U)   /∴   **U**
    4. ~I   3   Simp
    5. M   1,4   DS
    6. T   2,5   MP
    7. (T ⊃ U) · ~I   3   Com
    8. T ⊃ U   7   Simp
    9. U   8,6   MP

4. **1. ~(A · B)**   /∴   **B ⊃ ~A**

    2. ~A ∨ ~B   1   DeM
    3. ~B ∨ ~A   2   Com
    4. B ⊃ ~A   3   MI

5.   **1. S ∨ (F · M)**
    2. S ⊃ F
    3. J ≡ S
    4. J ⊃ ~T   /∴   **~T ≡ S**

    INVALID: **S F M J T**
                   F T T F F

6.   **1. D ⊃ F**
    2. F ⊃ K
    3. K ⊃ M
    4. ~M   /∴   **~D**
    5. ~K   3,4   MT
    6. ~F   2,5   MT
    7. ~D   1,6   MT

7.   **1. P ⊃ I**
    2. P ∨ L
    3. L ⊃ R
    4. ~R   /∴   **P · I**
    5. ~L   3,4   MT
    6. L ∨ P   2   Com
    7. P   6,5   DS
    8. I   1,7   MP
    9. P · I   7,8   Conj

8.   **1. ~(D ∨ T)**
    2. ~D ⊃ B
    3. M ⊃ ~B   /∴   **~M**
    4. ~D · ~T   1   DeM
    5. ~D   4   Simp
    6. B   2,5   MP

7. B ⊃ ~M	3	Transp
8. ~M	7,6	MP

9.
1. **~S ⊃ B**		
2. **S ⊃ ~F**	/∴	**B ∨ ~F**
3. ~B ⊃ S	1	Transp
4. ~B ⊃ ~F	3,2	HS
5. B ∨ ~F	4	MI

10.
1. **T ⊃ S**		
2. **~S ∨ R**		
3. **~R ∨ C**	/∴	**T ⊃ C**
4. S ⊃ R	2	MI
5. R ⊃ C	3	MI
6. T ⊃ R	1,4	HS
7. T ⊃ C	6,5	HS

11.
1. **~T ⊃ E**		
2. **T ∨ L**	/∴	**~E ⊃ ~L**

INVALID: **T E L**
           T F T

12.
1. **F ⊃ G**		
2. **F ⊃ (G ⊃ C)**		
3. **(F ⊃ C) ≡ S**	/∴	**(S · C) ⊃ F**

INVALID: **F G C S**
           F T T T

13.
1. **O ⊃ P**		
2. **~C ⊃ ~P**		
3. **O ∨ ~P**	/∴	**O ≡ C**

INVALID: **O P C**
           F F T

14. 1. C ≡ S
    2. ~S ∨ M
    3. (C ⊃ M) ⊃ P   /∴   P
    4. (C ⊃ S) · (S ⊃ C)   1   MEA
    5. S ⊃ M   2   MI
    6. C ⊃ S   4   Simp
    7. C ⊃ M   6,5   HS
    8. P   3,7   MP

15. 1. A ⊃ (B ⊃ S)
    2. B ≡ L
    3. ~S ∨ L   /∴   L ≡ S

    INVALID: A B S L
               F T F T

16. 1. L ⊃ U
    2. L ∨ ~F
    3. ~~F   /∴   U
    4. ~F ∨ L   2   Com
    5. L   4,3   DS
    6. U   1,5   MP

17. 1. A ⊃ D
    2. D ≡ B
    3. ~B ∨ N   /∴   (N · D) ⊃ A

    INVALID: A D B N
               F T T T

18. 1. C ⊃ D
    2. C ⊃ (D ⊃ L)
    3. (C ⊃ D) ≡ G   /∴   (G · L) ⊃ D

    INVALID: C D L G
               F F T T

19. **1. (O ⊃ T) · (~O ⊃ K)**
    2. ~K /∴ **T**
    3. (~O ⊃ K) · (O ⊃ T)   1   Com
    4. ~O ⊃ K   3   Simp
    5. ~~O   4,2   MT
    6. O   5   DN
    7. O ⊃ T   1   Simp
    8. T   7,6   MP

20. **1. M ⊃ (L · E)**
    2. L ⊃ W /∴ **M ⊃ W**
    3. ~M ∨ (L · E)   1   MI
    4. (~M ∨ L) · (~M ∨ E)   3   Dist
    5. ~M ∨ L   4   Simp
    6. M ⊃ L   5   MI
    7. M ⊃ W   6,2   HS

21. **1. M ⊃ L**
    2. M ∨ T
    3. T ⊃ C
    4. ~C /∴ **L**
    5. ~T   3,4   MT
    6. M   2,5   DS
    7. L   1,6   MP

22. **1. ~P ∨ S**
    2. ~S
    3. E ⊃ (~P ⊃ F) /∴ **E ⊃ F**
    4. S ∨ ~P   1   Com
    5. ~P   4,2   DS
    6. (E · ~P) ⊃ F   3   Exp
    7. (~P · E) ⊃ F   6   Com
    8. ~P ⊃ (E ⊃ F)   7   Exp
    9. E ⊃ F   8,5   MP

23. **1. S ⊃ P**
    2. ~P ∨ O
    3. O ≡ G   /∴   **(S ∨ D) ⊃ G**

    INVALID: **S P O G D**
               F F F F T

24. **1. F ∨ B**
    2. G ⊃ ~B
    3. (~F ⊃ ~G) ⊃ D
    4. ~D ∨ S   /∴   **S**
    5. ~F ⊃ B   1   MI
    6. B ⊃ ~G   2   Transp
    7. ~F ⊃ ~G   5,6   HS
    8. D   3,7   MP
    9. D ⊃ S   4   MI
    10. S   9,8   MP

25. **1. (~I ⊃ C) · (I ⊃ K)**   /∴   **C ∨ K**
    2. ~I ⊃ C   1   Simp
    3. I ⊃ K   1   Simp
    4. ~C ⊃ I   2   Transp
    5. ~C ⊃ K   4,3   HS
    6. C ∨ K   5   MI

26. **1. D ∨ (P · B)**
    2. (D ∨ B) ⊃ G
    3. ~G ∨ L   /∴   **L**
    4. (D ∨ P) · (D ∨ B)   1   Distrb
    5. D ∨ B   4   Simp
    6. G   2,5   MP
    7. G ⊃ L   3   MI
    8. L   7,6   MP

27. **1. S ⊃ W**
    2. A ≡ W

      3. A ⊃ G
      4. G ⊃ B   /∴   **S ⊃ B**
      5. (A ⊃ W) · (W ⊃ A)   2   MEA
      6. W ⊃ A   5   Simp
      7. S ⊃ A   1,6 HS
      8. S ⊃ G   7,3 HS
      9. S ⊃ B   8,4 HS

28. 1. I ⊃ (K · B)
      2. (~I ∨ B) ⊃ T
      3. ~T ∨ U   /∴   **U**
      4. ~I ∨ (K · B)   1   MI
      5. (~I ∨ K) · (~I ∨ B) 4   Distrb
      6. ~I ∨ B   5   Simp
      7. T   2,6 MP
      8. T ⊃ U   3   MI
      9. U   8,7 MP

29. 1. F · S
      2. (F · S) ⊃ (Y ≡ M)
      3. T
      4. ~(T · M)   /∴   **~Y**
      5. ~T ∨ ~M   4   DeM
      6. T ⊃ ~M   5   MI
      7. ~M   6,3 MP
      8. Y ≡ M   2,1 MP
      9. (Y ⊃ M) · (M ⊃ Y) 8   MEA
    10. Y ⊃ M   9   Simp
    11. ~Y   10,7 MT

30. 1. G ∨ (N · M)
      2. (N ⊃ ~M) · A
      3. (W ∨ K) ⊃ ~G
      4. ~(W ∨ K) ⊃ S   /∴   **S**
      5. N ⊃ ~M   2   Simp

6.	~N ∨ ~M	5	MI
7.	~(N · M)	6	DeM
8.	(N · M) ∨ G	1	Com
9.	G	8,7	DS
10.	~~G	9	DN
11.	~(W ∨ K)	3,10	MT
13.	S	4,11	MP

31.	**1. H ⊃ T**		
	2. H ⊃ (T ⊃ C)		
	3. ~(H ⊃ C) ∨ E		
	4. E ⊃ (P ∨ N)		
	5. ~P	/∴	**N**
	6. H ⊃ (H · T)	1	Abs
	7. (H · T) ⊃ C	2	Exp
	8. H ⊃ C	6,7	HS
	9. (H ⊃ C) ⊃ E	3	MI
	10. E	9,8	MP
	11. P ∨ N	4,10	MP
	12. N	11,5	DS

32.	**1. J ≡ M**		
	2. ~J · M	/∴	**S**
	3. (J ⊃ M) · (M ⊃ J)	1	MEA
	4. (M ⊃ J) · (J ⊃ M)	3	Com
	5. M ⊃ J	4	Simp
	6. ~J	2	Simp
*7.	~M	5,6	MT
	8. M · ~J	2	Com
*9.	M	8	Simp
	10. M ∨ S	9	Add
	11. S	10,7	DS

*Valid but not sound. Inconsistent premises.

33.	**1. T ⊃ Q**	
	2. T ∨ (A · W)	

3. ~(A ∨ S)

4. W ⊃ N	/∴	**Q ∨ N**	
5. (T ∨ A) · (T ∨ W)	2	Distrb	
6. (T ∨ W) · (T ∨ A)	5	Com	
7. T ∨ W	6	Simp	
8. (T ⊃ Q) · (W ⊃ N)	1,4	Conj	
9. Q ∨ N	8,7	CD	

Premise three is superfluous.

34. **1. I ∨ A**

2. A ⊃ H			
3. I ⊃ K	/∴	**H ∨ K**	
4. ~I ⊃ A	1	MI	
5. ~I ⊃ H	4,2	HS	
6. ~H ⊃ I	5	Transp	
7. ~H ⊃ K	6,3	HS	
8. H ∨ K	7	MI	

35. **1. (P ∨ C) ⊃ N**

	/∴	**C ⊃ (N ∨ B)**	
2. ~(P ∨ C) ∨ N	1	MI	
3. (~P · ~C) ∨ N	2	DeM	
4. N ∨ (~P · ~C)	3	Com	
5. (N ∨ ~P) · (N ∨ ~C)	4	Distrb	
6. (N ∨ ~C) · (N ∨ ~P)	5	Com	
7. N ∨ ~C	6	Simp	
8. ~C ∨ N	7	Com	
9. (~C ∨ N) ∨ B	8	Add	
10. ~C ∨ (N ∨ B)	9	Assc	
11. C ⊃ (N ∨ B)	10	MI	

36. **1. S ∨ (C · D)**

2. C ⊃ (D ⊃ N)			
3. ~(N · S)	/∴	**~N ≡ S**	
4. ~N ∨ ~S	3	DeM	
5. ~S ∨ ~N	4	Com	

6. S ⊃ ~N	5	MI
7. (C · D) ⊃ N	2	Exp
8. ~S ⊃ (C · D)	1	MI
9. ~S ⊃ N	8,7	HS
10. ~N ⊃ S	9	Transp
11. (~N ⊃ S) · (S ⊃ ~N)	10,6	Conj
12. ~N ≡ S	11	MEA

37.

1. (P ⊃ H) · (A ⊃ B)	/∴	**(P · A) ⊃ (H · B)**
2. P · A		
3. P	2	Simp
4. P ⊃ H	1	Simp
5. H	4,3	MP
6. A ⊃ B	1	Simp
7. A	2	Simp
8. B	6,7	MP
9. H · B	5,8	Conj
10. (P · A) ⊃ (H · B)	2-9	CP

Without CP, it takes only three more lines; but they are harder to see.

2. (~P ∨ H) · (~A ∨ B)	1	MI
3. ~P ∨ H	2	Simp
4. ~A ∨ (~P ∨ H)	3	Add
5. (~A ∨ ~P) ∨ H	4	Assc
6. (~P ∨ ~A) ∨ H	5	Com
7. ~A ∨ B	2	Simp
8. ~P ∨ (~A ∨ B)	7	Add
9. (~P ∨ ~A) ∨ B	8	Assc
10. [(~P ∨ ~A) ∨ H] · [(~P ∨ ~A) ∨ B]	6,9	Conj
11. (~P ∨ ~A) ∨ (H · B)	10	Dist
12. ~(P · A) ∨ (H · B)	11	DeM
13. (P · A) ⊃ (H · B)	12	MI

38. **1.** [(E · S) ⊃ P] · [(E · ~S) ⊃ ~P]

/∴ E ⊃ [(S · P) ∨ (~S · ~P)]

   2. [E ⊃ (S ⊃ P)] · [E ⊃ (~S ⊃ ~P)]   1   Exp
   3. [~E ∨ (S ⊃ P)] · [~E ∨ (~S ⊃ ~P)]   2   MI
   4. ~E ∨ [(S ⊃ P) · (~S ⊃ ~P)]   3   Dist
   5. ~E ∨ [(S ⊃ P) · (P ⊃ S)]   4   Transp
   6. ~E ∨ (S ≡ P)   5   MEA
   7. ~E ∨ [(S · P) ∨ (~S · ~P)]   6   MEB
   8. E ⊃ [(S · P) ∨ (~S · ~P)]   7   MI

39. **1.** (~U ∨ T) · (S ⊃ U)   /∴   (P · S) ⊃ T
   2. ~U ∨ T   1   Simp
   3. (S ⊃ U) · (~U ∨ T)   1   Com
   4. S ⊃ U   3   Simp
   5. U ⊃ T   2   MI
   6. S ⊃ T   4,5 HS
   7. ~S ∨ T   6   MI
   8. (~S ∨ T) ∨ ~P   7   Add
   9. ~P ∨ (~S ∨ T)   8   Com
  10. (~P ∨ ~S) ∨ T   9   Assc
  11. ~(P · S) ∨ T   10   DeM
  12. (P · S) ⊃ T   11   MI

40. **1.** (S ⊃ D) · [S ⊃ (D ⊃ E)]
   2. (S ⊃ E) ⊃ B
   3. B ≡ R   /∴   R
   4. S ⊃ D   1   Simp
   5. [S ⊃ (D ⊃ E)] · (S ⊃ D)   1   Com
   6. S ⊃ (D ⊃ E)   5 · Simp
   7. S ⊃ (S · D)   4   Abs
   8. (S · D) ⊃ E   6   Export
   9. S ⊃ E   7,8 HS
  10. B   2,9 MP
  11. (B ⊃ R) · (R ⊃ B)   3   MEA
  12. B ⊃ R   11   Simp
  13. R   12,10 MP

41. 1. S ⊃ F
     2. (F ∨ D) ⊃ ~S
     3. W ⊃ (H · S)
     4. W   /∴   B
     5. H · S   3,4   MP
     6. S · H   5   Com
    *7. S   6   Simp
     8. F   1,7   MP
     9. F ∨ D   8   Add
   *10. ~S   2,9   MP
     11. S ∨ B   7   Add
     12. B   11,10 D S

*Valid but not sound; inconsistent premises.

42. 1. (M ⊃ A) · (S ⊃ A)
     2. A ⊃ P   /∴   ~P ⊃ ~(M ∨ S)
     3. ~A ⊃ ~M) · (~A ⊃ ~S) 1   Transp
     4. (A ∨ ~M) · (A ∨ ~S)   3   MI
     5. A ∨ (~M · ~S)   4   Dist
     6. ~A ⊃ (~M · ~S)   5   MI
     7. ~P ⊃ ~A   2   Transp
     8. ~P ⊃ (~M · ~S)   7,6 HS
     9. ~P ⊃ ~(M ∨ S)   8   DeM

43. 1. P ⊃ (L ∨ C)
     2. C ⊃ (O ⊃ ~P)
     3. C ⊃ (O ∨ B)
     4. ~X ⊃ ~B
     5. ~X   /∴   ~L ⊃ (~P · ~C)

INVALID   P L C O B X
           F F T T F F

44. 1. (I · S) ⊃ (G · P)
     2. [(S · ~I) ⊃ E] · (E ⊃ P)
     3. I ⊃ S   /∴   P

INVALID: **I S G P E**
          F F T F F

45. **1 . A ⊃ (B · C)**
    2. (B ∨ C) ⊃ F
    3. F ⊃ M   /∴   **A ⊃ M**
    4. (B ∨ C) ⊃ M   2,3   H S
    5. ~A ∨ (B · C)   1   MI
    6. (~A ∨ B) · (~A ∨ C)   5   Dist
    7. ~A ∨ B   6   Simp
    8. (~A ∨ B) ∨ C   7   Add
    9. ~A ∨ (B ∨ C)   8   Assc
    10. A ⊃ (B ∨ C)   9   MI
    11. A ⊃ M   10,4   H S

46. **1. (W ∨ E) · ~(W · E)**   /∴   **W ≡ ~E**
    2. W ∨ E   1   Simp
    3. E ∨ W   2   Com
    4. ~E ⊃ W   3   MI
    5. ~(W · E)   1   Simp
    6. ~W ∨ ~E   5   DeM
    7. W ⊃ ~E   6   MI
    8. (W ⊃ ~E) · (~E ⊃ W)   7,4   Conj
    9. W ≡ ~E   8   MEA

47. **1 . C ⊃ N**
    2. C ⊃ (N ⊃ E)
    3. (C ⊃ E) ⊃ R
    4. R ≡ H   /∴   **H**
    5. C ⊃ (C · N)   1   Abs
    6. (C · N) ⊃ E   2   Exp
    7. C ⊃ E   5,6   H S
    8. R   3,7   MP
    9. (R ⊃ H) · (H ⊃ R)   4   MEA
    10. R ⊃ H   9   Simp
    11. H   10,8   MP

48. 1. **(A · B) ⊃ C**
    2. **(C ∨ D) ⊃ (F ∨ L)**   /∴   **(~L · A) ⊃ F**

    INVALID: **A B C D F L**
              T F F F F F

49. 1. **V ∨ (E ≡ N)**
    2. **L ≡ ~V**
    3. **[(L · E) ⊃ N] ⊃ D**   /∴   **D**
    4. V ∨ [(E ⊃ N) · (N ⊃ E)]   1   MEA
    5. [V ∨ (E ⊃ N)] · [V ∨ (N ⊃ E)]   4   Distr
    6. V ∨ (E ⊃ N)   5   Simp
    7. ~V ⊃ (E ⊃ N)   6   MI
    8. (L ⊃ ~V) · (~V ⊃ L)   2   MEA
    9. L ⊃ ~V   8   Simp
    10. L ⊃ (E ⊃ N)   9,7   HS
    11. (L · E) ⊃ N   10   Exp
    12. D   3,11 MP

50. 1. **(D · E) ⊃ F**
    2. **D ⊃ (L · I)**   /∴   **(E · D) ⊃ (F · I)**
    3. E · D
    4. D · E   3   Com
    5. F   1,4   MP
    6. D   4   Simp
    7. L · I   2,6   MP
    8. I   7   Simp
    9. F · I   5,8   Conj
    10. (E · D) ⊃ (F · I)   3-9   CP

    With slightly greater ingenuity (and without CP):

    3. (E · D) ⊃ F   1   Com
    4. ~D ∨ (L · I)   2   MI
    5. (~D ∨ L) · (~D ∨ I)   4   Dist
    6. ~D ∨ I   6   Simp
    7. ~E ∨ (~D ∨ I)   6   Add

8. (~E ∨ ~D) ∨ I	7	Assc
9. ~(E · D) ∨ I	8	DeM
10. ~(E · D) ∨ F	3	MI
11. [~(E · D) ∨ F] · [~(E · D) ∨ I]	10,9	Conj
12. ~(E · D) ∨ (F · I)	11	Distrb
13. (E · D) ⊃ (F · I)	12	MI

51. **1. R ⊃ (T · C)**
    2. G ⊃ (B · F)
    3. (T · B) ⊃ ~D   /∴   **(R · G) ⊃ ~D**

4. R · G		
5. R	4	Simp
6. T · C	1,5	MP
7. T	6	Simp
8. G	4	Simp
9. B · F	2,8	MP
10. B	9	Simp
11. T · B	7,10	Conj
12. ~D	3,11	MP
13. (R · G) ⊃ ~D	4-12	CP

Exporting and commuting often help when manipulating complex chains.

4. ~R ∨ (T · C)	1	MI
5. (~R ∨ T) · (~R ∨ C)	4	Distr
6. ~R ∨ T	5	Simp
7. ~G ∨ (B · F)	2	MI
8. (~G ∨ B) · (~G ∨ F)	7	Distr
9. ~G ∨ B	8	Simp
10. R ⊃ T	6	MI
11. G ⊃ B	9	MI
12. T ⊃ (B ⊃ ~D)	3	Exp
13. R ⊃ (B ⊃ ~D)	10,12	HS
14. (R · B) ⊃ ~D	13	Exp
15. (B · R) ⊃ ~D	14	Com
16. B ⊃ (R ⊃ ~D)	15	Exp

17. G ⊃ (R ⊃ ~D)   11,16 HS
18. (G · R) ⊃ ~D   17   Exp
19. (R · G) ⊃ ~D   18   Com

52. 1. C ⊃ (L · R)
     2. L ⊃ ~(P ∨ D)
     3. ~D ≡ A   /∴   (R · P) ⊃ A

     INVALID: C L R P D A
                F F T T T F

53. 1. (P ⊃ S) · (F ⊃ ~H)
     2. P ⊃ (S ⊃ F)
     3. H ∨ (P · ~V)   /∴   P ≡ F
     4. P ⊃ S   1   Simp
     5. F ⊃ ~H   1   Simp
     6. P ⊃ (P · S)   4   Abs
     7. (P · S) ⊃ F   2   exp
     8. P ⊃ F   6,7   HS
     9. (H ∨ P) · (H ∨ ~V)   3   Dist
    10. H ∨ P   9   Simp
    11. ~H ⊃ P   10   MI
    12. F ⊃ P   5,11   HS
    13. (P ⊃ F) · (F ⊃ P)   8,12   Conj
    14. P ≡ F   13   MEA

54. 1. (N · K) ∨ S
     2. ~S ∨ (F · C)   /∴   (N ∨ K) · (F ∨ C)

     INVALID: N K S F C
                T T F F F

55. 1. S ∨ E
     2. (~S ⊃ E) ⊃ G
     3. (G · M) ≡ W
     4. C ∨ (S · ~W)   /∴   M ⊃ C

5. ~S ⊃ E	1	MI
6. G	2,5	MP
7. [(G · M) ⊃ W] · [W ⊃ (G · M)	3	MEA
8. (G · M) ⊃ W	7	Simp
9. G ⊃ (M ⊃ W)	8	Exp
10. M ⊃ W	9,6	MP
11. (C ∨ S) · (C ∨ ~W)	4	Dist
12. C ∨ ~W	11	Simp
13. ~W ∨ C	12	Com
14. W ⊃ C	13	MI
15. M ⊃ C	10,14	HS

56. 1. **H ⊃ (F ⊃ B)**
    2. **H ⊃ F**
    3. **(H ⊃ B) ⊃ C**
    4. **B ∨ D**   /∴   **D ⊃ ~C**

    INVALID: **H F B C D**
                   T T T T T

57. 1. **(P ⊃ A) · (G ⊃ C)**
    2. **~V ∨ (P ∨ G)**   /∴   **V ⊃ (A ∨ C)**

3. V		
4. V ⊃ (P ∨ G)	2	MI
5. P ∨ G	4,3	MP
6. A ∨ C	1,5	CD
7. V ⊃ (A ∨ C)	3-6	CP

Without the constructive dilemma that CP provides, the proof is much longer:

3. (~P ∨ A) · (~G ∨ C)	1	MI
4. ~P ∨ A	3	Simp
5. (~P ∨ A) ∨ C	4	Add
6. ~P ∨ (A ∨ C)	5	Assc
7. ~G ∨ C	3	Simp
8. (~G ∨ C) ∨ A	7	Add

9. ~G ∨ (C ∨ A)	8	Assc
10. ~G ∨ (A ∨ C)	9	Com
11. [~P ∨ (A ∨ C)] · [~G ∨ (A ∨ C)]	6,10	Conj
12. [(A ∨ C) ∨ ~P] · [(A ∨ C) ∨ ~G]	11	Com
13. (A ∨ C) ∨ (~P · ~G)	12	Dist
14. (~P · ~G) ∨ (A ∨ C)	13	Com
15. ~(P ∨ G) ∨ (A ∨ C)	14	DeM
16. (P ∨ G) ⊃ (A ∨ C)	15	MI
17. V ⊃ (P ∨ G)	2	MI
18. V ⊃ (A ∨ C)	17,16	HS

58.
1. **(M ∨ H) ⊃ (B · F)**
2. **(B ∨ F) ⊃ (S · C)**   /∴   **H ⊃ C**

3. H		
4. M ∨ H	3	Add
5. B · F	1,4	MP
6. B	5	Simp
7. B ∨ F	6	Add
8. S · C	2,7	MP
9. C	8	Simp
10. H ⊃ C	3-9	CP

Without CP, but with three applications of distribution and simplification, you can establish this in under twenty steps.

59.
1. **R ⊃ B**
2. **H ⊃ B**
3. **B ⊃ C**   /∴   **~C ⊃ ~(R ∨ H)**

4. (R ⊃ B) · (H ⊃ B)	1,2	Conj
5. (~B ⊃ ~R) · (~B ⊃ ~H)	4	Transp
6. (B ∨ ~R) · (B ∨ ~H)	5	MI
7. B ∨ (~R · ~H)	6	Dist
8. ~B ⊃ (~R · ~H)	7	MI
9. ~C ⊃ ~B	3	Transp

10. ~C ⊃ (~R · ~H)	9,8	HS
11. ~C ⊃ ~(R ∨ H)	10	DeM

Using CP only saves one line; but it is much more obvious:

4. ~C		
5. ~B	3,4	MT
6. ~H	2,5	MT
7. ~R	1,6	MT
8. ~R · ~H	7,6	Conj
9. ~(R ∨ H)	8	DeM
10. ~C ⊃ ~(R ∨ H)	4-9	CP

60. **1. (A ⊃ ~B) · (C ⊃ D)**
    2. (A ∨ C) · ~(B ≡ ~D)   /∴   **D · ~B**

    INVALID: **A B C D**
    　　　　　F T T T

61. **1. (V ⊃ E) · V**
    2. (E ⊃ S) · [S ⊃ (F · B)]
    3. (V · E) ⊃ ~B   /∴   **V ≡ ~S**

4. V ⊃ E	1	Simp
5. V	1	Simp
6. E	4,5	MP
7. V · E	5,6	Conj
* 8. ~B	3,7	MP
9. E ⊃ S	2	Simp
10. S	9,6	MP
11. S ⊃ (F · B)	2	Simp
12. F · B	11,10	MP
*13. B	12	Simp
14. B ∨ (V ≡ ~S)	13	Add
15. V ≡ ~S	14,8	DS

*Valid but not sound; inconsistent premises.

62. 1. F ⊃ R
     2. F ⊃ (R ⊃ E)
     3. (F ⊃ E) ⊃ P
     4. ~(P ∨ L)   /∴   Y
     5. F ⊃ (F · R)   1   Abs
     6. (F · R) ⊃ E   2   Export
     7. F ⊃ E   5,6   HS
   *8. P   3,7   MP
     9. ~P · ~L   4   DeM
  *10. ~P   9   Simp
    11. P ∨ Y   8   Add
    12. Y   11,10 D S

   *Valid but not sound; inconsistent premises.

63. 1. P ⊃ (Q · R)
     2. (S ∨ Q) ⊃ T   /∴   P ⊃ T
     3. ~P ∨ (Q · R)   1   MI
     4. (~P ∨ Q) · (~P ∨ R)   3   Dist
     5. ~P ∨ Q   4   Simp
     6. (~P ∨ Q) ∨ S   5   Add
     7. ~P ∨ (Q ∨ S)   6   Assc
     8. ~P ∨ (S ∨ Q)   7   Com
     9. P ⊃ (S ∨ Q)   8   MI
    10. P ⊃ T   9,2   HS

64. 1. ~A ∨ (D · P)
     2. C ≡ S
     3. ~(D · C)   /∴   S ⊃ ~A
     4. ~D ∨ ~C   3   DeM
     5. (~A ∨ D) · (~A ∨ P)   1   Dist
     6. ~A ∨ D   5   Simp
     7. A ⊃ D   6   MI
     8. D ⊃ ~C   4   MI
     9. A ⊃ ~C   7,8   HS
    10. (C ⊃ S) · (S ⊃ C)   2   MEA

11. S ⊃ C	10	Simp
12. C ⊃ ~A	9	Transp
13. S ⊃ ~A	11,12	HS

65. **1. P ∨ (S · T)**
    2. ~(S ∨ M)

3. ~M ⊃ A	/∴	**P ≡ A**
4. ~S · ~M	2	DeM
5. (P ∨ S) · (P ∨ T)	1	Dist
6. P ∨ S	5	Simp
7. ~S	4	Simp
8. P	6,7	DS
9. ~M	4	Simp
10. A	3,9	MP
11. P · A	8,10	Conj
12. (P · A) ∨ (~P · ~A)	11	Add
13. P ≡ A	12	MEB

66. **1. G ∨ (E · I)**
    2. O ⊃ (S ≡ P)
    3. (P ⊃ S) ⊃ (R ⊃ ~G)

4. I ⊃ F	/∴	**O ⊃ (R ⊃ F)**
5. O		
6. S ≡ P	2,5	MP
7. (S ⊃ P) · (P ⊃ S)	6	MEA
8. P ⊃ S	7	Simp
9. R ⊃ ~G	3,8	MP
10. (G ∨ E) · (G ∨ I)	1	Dist
11. G ∨ I	10	Simp
12. ~G ⊃ I	11	MI
13. ~G ⊃ F	12,4	HS
14. R ⊃ F	9,13	HS
15. O ⊃ (R ⊃ F)	5-14	CP

67. **1. K ⊃ (A · B)**
    2. (I ∨ A) ⊃ T

3. (K ⊃ T) ⊃ ~P	/∴	**~P**

4. ~K ∨ (A · B)	1	MI
5. (~K ∨ A) · (~K ∨ B)	4	Dist
6. ~K ∨ A	5	Simp
7. (~K ∨ A) ∨ I	6	Add
8. ~K ∨ (A ∨ I)	7	Assc
9. ~K ∨ (I ∨ A)	8	Com
10. K ⊃ (I ∨ A)	9	MI
11. K ⊃ T	10,2	HS
12. ~P	3,11	MP

But you can save two lines with a conditional proof:

4. K		
5. A · B	1,4	MP
6. A	5	Simp
7. I ∨ A	6	Add
8. T	2,7	MP
9. K ⊃ T	4-8	CP
10. ~P	3,9	MP

68. 1. K ≡ (P ∨ A)
    2. F ⊃ ~K
    3. [(L · ~K) · (~A · P)] ⊃ H   /∴   F ⊃ H

    INVALID: **K P A F L H**
               F F F T T F

69. 1. (M ∨ T) ⊃ P   /∴   T ⊃ {P ∨ [R ∨ (B ∨ A)]}
    2. ~(M ∨ T) ∨ P   1   MI
    3. P ∨ ~(M ∨ T)   2   Com
    4. P ∨ (~M · ~T)   3   DeM
    5. (P ∨ ~M) · (P ∨ ~T)   4   Dist
    6. P ∨ ~T   5   Simp
    7. ~T ∨ P   6   Com
    8. (~T ∨ P) ∨ [R ∨ (B ∨ A)]   7   Add
    9. ~T ∨ {P ∨ [R ∨ (B ∨ A)]}   8   Assc
    10. T ⊃ {P ∨ [R ∨ (B ∨ A)]}   9   MI

Using Conditional Proof nearly cuts it in half:

2. T		
3. M ∨ T	2	Add
4. P	1,3	MP
5. P ∨ [R ∨ (B ∨ A)]	4	Add
6. T ⊃ {P ∨ [R ∨ (B ∨ A)]}	2-5	CP

70. **1. G ⊃ (F ⊃ P)**
    2. B ⊃ (G · F)
    3. T ∨ B
    4. T ∨ A
    5. ~P /∴ **~F ∨ A**

    INVALID: **G F P B T A**
            F T F F T F

71. **1. B ∨ U**
    2. (J ⊃ R) · (~J ⊃ S)
    3. (R ∨ S) ⊃ ~B /∴ **U ∨ E**
    4. J ⊃ R   2   Simp
    5. ~J ⊃ S   2   Simp
    6. ~R ⊃ ~J   4   Transp
    7. ~R ⊃ S   6,5   HS
    8. R ∨ S   7   MI
    9. ~B   3,8   MP
    10. U   1,9   DS
    11. U ∨ E   10   Add

72. **1. (F ∨ M) ⊃ A** /∴ **(F · M) ⊃ A**
    2. ~(F ∨ M) ∨ A   1   MI
    3. (~F · ~M) ∨ A   2   DeM
    4. A ∨ (~F · ~M)   3   Com
    5. (A ∨ ~F) · (A ∨ ~M)   4   Dist
    6. A ∨ ~F   5   Simp
    7. (A ∨ ~F) ∨ ~M   6   Add
    8. A ∨ (~F ∨ ~M)   7   Assc

	9. (~F ∨ ~M) ∨ A	8	Com
	10. ~(F · M) ∨ A	9	DeM
	11. (F · M) ⊃ A	10	MI

73.
1. **(M ⊃ F) · (T ⊃ H)**
2. **M ∨ T**
3. **(F ∨ H) ⊃ S**
4. **S ≡ Q**   /∴   **Q u C**
5. F ∨ H   1,2   CD
6. S   3,5   MP
7. (S ⊃ Q) · (Q ⊃ S)   4   MEA
8. S ⊃ Q   7   Simp
9. Q   8,6   MP
10. Q ∨ C   9   Add

74.
1. **A ⊃ B**
2. **W ≡ A**
3. **~B ∨ T**
4. **~W ⊃ T**   /∴   **T**
5. B ⊃ T   3   MI
6. A ⊃ T   1,5   HS
7. (W ⊃ A) · (A ⊃ W)   2   MEA
8. W ⊃ A   7   Simp
9. ~A ⊃ ~W   8   Trans
10. ~A ⊃ T   9,4   HS
11. ~T ⊃ ~A   6   Trans
12. ~T ⊃ T   11,10 HS
13. T ∨ T   12   MI
14. T   13   Taut

75.
1. **A · (B ∨ H)**
2. **~X ∨ (M · ~S)**
3. **(A · H) ⊃ X**
4. **(~S ∨ W) ⊃ (F ≡ C)**   /∴   **~(A · B) ⊃ (C ⊃ F)**
5. ~(A · B)
6. (A · B) ∨ (A · H)   1   Dist

7. A · H	6,5	DS
8. X	3,7	MP
9. X ⊃ (M · ~S)	2	MI
10. M · ~S	9,8	MP
11. ~S	10	Simp
12. ~S ∨ W	11	Add
13. F ≡ C	4,12	MP
14. (F ⊃ C) · (C ⊃ F)	13	MEA
15. C ⊃ F	15	Simp
16. ~(A · B) ⊃ (C ⊃ F)	5-15	CP

Without conditional proof, it can be done this way:

5. (A · B) ∨ (A · H)	1	Dist
6. ~(A · B) ⊃ (A · H)	5	MI
7. ~(A · B) ⊃ X	6,3	HS
8. X ⊃ (M · ~S)	2	MI
9. ~(A · B) ⊃ (M · ~S)	7,8	HS
10. (A · B) ∨ (M · ~S)	9	MI
11. [(A · B) ∨ M] · [(A · B) ∨ ~S]	10	Dist
12. (A · B) ∨ ~S	11	Simp
13. [(A · B) ∨ ~S] ∨ W	12	Add
14. (A · B) ∨ (~S ∨ W)	13	Assc
15. ~(A · B) ⊃ (~S ∨ W)	14	MI
16. ~(A · B) ⊃ (F ≡ C)	15,4	HS
17. ~(A · B) ⊃ [(F ⊃ C) · (C ⊃ F)]	16	MEA
18. (A · B) ∨ [(F ⊃ C) · (C ⊃ F)]	17	MI
19. [(A · B) ∨ (F ⊃ C)] · [(A · B) ∨ (C ⊃ F)]	18	Dist
20. (A · B) ∨ (C ⊃ F)	19	Simp
21. ~(A · B) ⊃ (C ⊃ F)	20	MI

76.
1. **M ≡ (S · N)**		
2. **N ⊃ (S ∨ D)**	/∴	**[(~D · ~F) · N] ⊃ (S · M)**
3. (~D · ~F) · N		
4. N · (~D · ~F)	3	Com
5. N	4	Simp

6. S ∨ D	2,5	MP
7. ~D · ~F	3	Simp
8. ~D	7	Simp
9. S	6,8	DS
10. S · N	9,5	Conj
11. [M ⊃ (S · N)] · [(S · N) ⊃ M]	1	MEA
12. [(S · N) ⊃ M] · [M ⊃ (S · N)]	12	Com
13. [(S · N) ⊃ M]	13	Simp
14. M	14,11	MP
15. S · M	9,15	Conj
16. [(~D · ~F) · N] ⊃ (S · M)	3-15	CP

77.

1. (M ⊃ L) · (T ⊃ B)		
2. S ∨ (M ∨ T)	/∴	**~S ⊃ (~L ⊃ B)**
3. ~S		
4. M ∨ T	2,3	DS
5. L ∨ B	1,4	CD
6. ~L ⊃ B	5	MI
7. ~S ⊃ (~L ⊃ B)	3-6	CP

Without conditional proof, it can be done this way.

3. (~M ∨ L) · (~T ∨ B)	1	MI
4. ~M ∨ L	3	Simp
5. (~M ∨ L) ∨ B	4	Add
6. ~M ∨ (L ∨ B)	5	Assc
7. ~T ∨ B	3	Simp
8. (~T ∨ B) ∨ L	7	Add
9. ~T ∨ (B ∨ L)	8	Assc
10. ~T ∨ (L ∨ B)	9	Com
11. [~M ∨ (L ∨ B)] · [~T ∨ (L ∨ B)]	6,10	Conj
12. [(L ∨ B) ∨ ~M] · [(L ∨ B) ∨ ~T]	11	Com
13. (L ∨ B) ∨ (~M · ~T)	12	Dist
14. (~M · ~T) ∨ (L ∨ B)	13	Com
15. ~(M ∨ T) ∨ (L ∨ B)	14	DeM
16. (M ∨ T) ⊃ (L ∨ B)	15	MI

17. ~S ⊃ (M ∨ T)	2	MI
18. ~S ⊃ (L ∨ B)	17,16	HS
19. ~S ⊃ (~L ⊃ B)	18	MI

78. **1. (A ⊃ R) · (B ⊃ W)**
    2. D ⊃ (A ∨ B)   /∴   **D ⊃ [~W ⊃ (R · A)]**

3. D		
4. ~W		
5. B ⊃ W	1	Simp
6. ~B	5,4	MT
7. A ∨ B	2,3	MP
8. A	7,6	DS
9. A ⊃ R	1	Simp
10. R	9,8	MP
11. R · A	10,8	Conj
12. ~W ⊃ (R · A)	4-11	CP
13. D ⊃ [~W ⊃ (R · A)]	3-12	CP

A straight proof is also worth the effort. How short can you make one? Just for fun, here is a reductio proof, too.

3. ~{D ⊃ [~W ⊃ (R · A)]}		
4. ~{~D ∨ [W ∨ (R · A)]}	3	MI
5. D · ~[W ∨ (R · A)]	4	DeM
6. D · [~W · ~(R · A)]	5	DeM
7. D	6	Simp
8. ~W · ~(R · A)	6	Simp
9. A ∨ B	2,7	MP
10. R ∨ W	1,9	CD
11. ~W	8	Simp
12. R	10,11	DS
13. ~(R · A)	8	Simp
14. ~R ∨ ~A	13	DeM
15. R ⊃ ~A	14	MI
16. ~A	15,12	MP
17. B	9,16	DS
18. B ⊃ W	1	Simp

	19. W	18,17 MP
	20. W · ~W	19,11 Conj
	21. D ⊃ [~W ⊃ (R · A)]	3-20 RAA

79. **1. B ⊃ ~S**
    2. A · K
    3. K ⊃ R
    4. H ≡ ~B   /∴   **(R ⊃ ~H) ∨ S**

    INVALID: **B S A K R H**
              F F T T T T

80. **1. R ⊃ (S ∨ T)**
    2. (S ∨ B) ⊃ R   /∴   **~T ⊃ (R ≡ S)**
    3. ~R ∨ (S ∨ T)   1   MI
    4. (~R ∨ S) ∨T   3   Assc
    5. T ∨ (~R ∨ S)   4   Com
    6. T ∨ (R ⊃ S)   5   MI
    7. ~R ⊃ ~(S ∨ B)   2   Transp
    8. R ∨ ~(S ∨ B)   7   MI
    9. R ∨ (~S · ~B)   8   DeM
    10. (R ∨ ~S) · (R ∨ ~B)   9   Dist
    11. R ∨ ~S   10   Simp
    12. ~R ⊃ ~S   11   MI
    13. S ⊃ R   12   Transp
    14. (S ⊃ R) ∨ T   13   Add
    15. T ∨ (S ⊃ R)   14   Com
    16. [T ∨ (R ⊃ S)] · [T ∨ (S ⊃ R)]   6,15   Conj
    17. T ∨ [(R ⊃ S) · (S ⊃ R)]   16   Dist
    18. T ∨ (R ≡ S)   17   MEA
    19. ~T ⊃ (R ≡ S)   18   MI

Of course you could do this by CP; but this is nicer.

81.
1. **Q ≡ ~S**
2. **P ⊃ (S ∨ K)**   /∴   **P ⊃ (Q ⊃ K)**
3. P ⊃ (~S ⊃ K)   2   MI
4. (P · ~S) ⊃ K   3   Export
5. (~S · P) ⊃ K   4   Com
6. ~S ⊃ (P ⊃ K)   5   Export
7. (Q ⊃ ~S) · (~S ⊃ Q)   1   MEA
8. Q ⊃ ~S   7   Simp
9. Q ⊃ (P ⊃ K)   8,6   HS
10. (Q · P) ⊃ K   9   Export
11. (P · Q) ⊃ K   10   Com
12. P ⊃ (Q ⊃ K)   11   Export

A nested conditional proof will also work; but it only saves a few lines.

82.
1. **(L ⊃ E) · (R ⊃ B)**
2. **(~B ∨ C) · (~E ∨ T)**   /∴   **(L ∨ R) ⊃ (C ∨ T)**
3. L ∨ R
4. E ∨ B   1,3   CD
5. (B ⊃ C) · (E ⊃ T)   2   MI
6. B ∨ E   4   Com
7. C ∨ T   5,6   CD
8. (L ∨ R) ⊃ (C ∨ T)   3-7   CP

A straight proof is tedious here. Can you construct one?

83.
1. **L**   /∴   **(P ≡ Q) ≡ [(P ∨ Q) ⊃ (P · Q)]**
2. P ≡ Q
3. (P · Q) ∨ (~P · ~Q)   2   MEB
4. (~P · ~Q) ∨ (P · Q)   3   Com
5. ~(P ∨ Q) ∨ (P · Q)   4   DeM
6. (P ∨ Q) ⊃ (P · Q)   5   MI
7. (P ≡ Q) ⊃ [(P ∨ Q) ⊃ (P · Q)]   2-6   CP
8. (P ∨ Q) ⊃ (P · Q)
9. ~(P ∨ Q) ∨ (P · Q)   8   MI
10. (~P · ~Q) ∨ (P · Q)   9   DeM

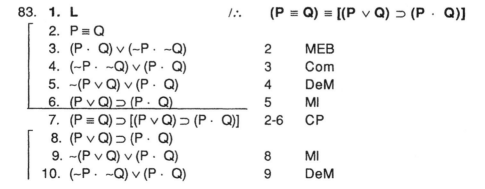

11. (P · Q) ∨ (~P · ~Q)	10	Com
12. P ≡ Q	11	MEB
13. [(P ∨ Q) ⊃ (P · Q)] ⊃ (P ≡ Q)	8-12	CP
14. {(P ≡ Q) ⊃ [(P ∨ Q) ⊃ (P · Q)]} · {[(P ∨ Q) ⊃ (P · Q)] ⊃ (P ≡ Q)}	7,13	Conj
15. (P ≡ Q) ≡ [(P ∨ Q) ⊃ (P · Q)]	14,	MEA

Surprisingly, a straight proof is no longer, but it is far more subtle. It involves absorbtion (common when generating tautologies without the help of any hypothesis).

2. (P ≡ Q) ∨ L	1	Add
3. ~(P ≡ Q) ⊃ L	2	MI
4. ~(P ≡ Q) ⊃ [~(P ≡ Q) · L]	3	Abs
5. (P ≡ Q) ∨ [~(P ≡ Q) · L]	4	MI
6. [(P ≡ Q) ∨ ~(P ≡ Q)] · [(P ≡ Q) ∨ L]	5	Dist
7. (P ≡ Q) ∨ ~(P ≡ Q)	6	Simp
8. ~(P ≡ Q) ∨ (P ≡ Q)	7	Com
9. (P ≡ Q) ⊃ (P ≡ Q)	8	MI
10. [(P ≡ Q) ⊃ (P ≡ Q)] · [(P ≡ Q) ⊃ (P ≡ Q)]	9	Taut
11. (P ≡ Q) ≡ (P ≡ Q)	10	MEA
12. (P ≡ Q) ≡ [(P · Q) ∨ (~P · ~Q)]	11	MEB
13. (P ≡ Q) ≡ [(~P · ~Q) ∨ (P · Q)]	12	Com
14. (P ≡ Q) ≡ [~(P ∨ Q) ∨ (P · Q)]	13	DeM
15. (P ≡ Q) ≡ [(P ∨ Q) ⊃ (P · Q)]	14	MI

Quite readily done by reductio, too. Since the conclusion is a tautology, its denial quickly yields a contradiction by repeated DeMorgan. There are many ways around this barn.

84.
1. ~M ⊃ ~A		
2. (~P ∨ S) · (S ⊃ A)		
3. ~P ⊃ (L · A)	/∴	M
4. P ∨ (L · A)	3	MI
5. (P ∨ L) · (P ∨ A)	4	Dist
6. P ∨ A	5	Simp
7. ~P ⊃ A	6	MI

8.	~P ∨ S	2	Simp
9.	P ⊃ S	8	MI
10.	S ⊃ A	2	Simp
11.	P ⊃ A	9,10,	HS
12.	~A ⊃ ~P	11	Transp
13.	~A ⊃ A	12,7	HS
14.	A ∨ A	13	MI
15.	A	14	Taut
16.	A ⊃ M	1	Transp
17.	M	16,15	MP

85.
1. **A ⊃ ~C**
2. **(~C · ~F) ⊃ S**
3. **(~F · S) ⊃ M**
4. **M ⊃ J**   /∴   **A ⊃ (S ⊃ J)**

INVALID: **A C F S M J**
          T F T T F F

86.
1. **~T ⊃ (F ∨ I)**
2. **G ⊃ ~F**
3. **C ⊃ (G · ~T)**   /∴   **C ⊃ I**

4.	C		
5.	G · ~T	3,4	MP
6.	G	5	Simp
7.	~F	2,6	MP
8.	~T	5	Simp
9.	F ∨ I	1,8	MP
10.	I	9,7	D S
11.	C ⊃ I	4-11	CP

Or, without the hypothesis:

4.	~C ∨ (G · ~T)	3	MI
5.	(~C ∨ G) · (~C ∨ ~T)	4	Dist
6.	~C ∨ ~T	5	Simp
7.	C ⊃ ~T	6	MI

8.	C ⊃ (F ∨ I)	7,1	HS
9.	~C ∨ (F ∨ I)	8	MI
10.	(F ∨ I) ∨ ~C	9	Com
11.	F ∨ (I ∨ ~C)	10	Assc
12.	F ∨ (~C ∨ I)	11	Com
13.	~F ⊃ (C ⊃ I)	12	MI
14.	~C ∨ G	5	Simp
15.	C ⊃ G	14	MI
16.	C ⊃ ~F	15,2	HS
17.	C ⊃ (C ⊃ I)	16,13	HS
18.	(C · C) ⊃ I	17	Export
19.	C ⊃ I	18	Taut

87.
1.	**E ⊃ I**		
2.	**~I ∨ W**		
3.	**W ≡ P**		
4.	**E ∨ R**		
5.	**R ⊃ (~S ∨ C)**		
6.	**S**	/∴	**P ∨ C**
7.	I ⊃ W	2	MI
8.	(W ⊃ P) · (P ⊃ W)	3	MEA
9.	W ⊃ P	8	Simp
10.	E ⊃ W	1,7	HS
11.	E ⊃ P	10,9	HS
12.	R ⊃ (S ⊃ C)	5	MI
13.	(R · S) ⊃ C	12	Exp
14.	(S · R) ⊃ C	13	Com
15.	S ⊃ (R ⊃ C)	14	Exp
16.	R ⊃ C	15,6	MP
17.	(E ⊃ P) · (R ⊃ C)	11,16	Conj
18.	P ∨ C	17,4	CD

88.
1.	**(B ⊃ C) · [(F · C) ⊃ A]**		
2.	**M ≡ (A ∨ B)**		
3.	**(~C ⊃ ~M) ⊃ P**	/∴	**~A ⊃ P**

4.	B ⊃ C	1	Simp
5.	[M ⊃ (A ∨ B)] · [(A ∨ B) ⊃ M]	2	MEA
6.	M ⊃ (A ∨ B)	5	Simp
7.	~M ∨ (A ∨ B)	6	MI
8.	(~M ∨ A) ∨ B	7	Assc
9.	(A ∨ ~M) ∨ B	8	Com
10.	A ∨ (~M ∨ B)	9	Assc
11.	~A ⊃ (M ⊃ B)	10	MI
12.	(~A · M) ⊃ B	11	Exp
13.	(~A · M) ⊃ C	12,4	HS
14.	~A ⊃ (M ⊃ C)	13	Exp
15.	~A ⊃ (~C ⊃ ~M)	14	Transp
16.	~A ⊃ P	15,3	HS

89.

1.	~H ∨ (S · P)		
2.	(P ∨ G) ≡ E		
3.	(E · I) ⊃ M		
4.	~M ∨ N	/∴	~H ∨ (I ⊃ N)
5.	H		
6.	H ⊃ (S · P)	1	MI
7.	S · P	6,5	MP
8.	P	7	Simp
9.	P ∨ G	8	Add
10.	[(P ∨ G) ⊃ E] · [E ⊃ (P ∨ G)]	2	MEA
11.	(P ∨ G) ⊃ E	10	Simp
12.	E	11,1	MP
13.	I		
14.	E · I	12,13	Conj
15.	M	3,14	MP
16.	M ⊃ N	4	MI
17.	N	16,15	MP
18.	I ⊃ N	13-17	CP
19.	H ⊃ (I ⊃ N)	5-18	CP
20.	~H ∨ (I ⊃ N)	19	MI

90.

1.	D ∨ (M · T)
2.	(D ∨ M) ⊃ S

3.	C ⊃ ~(S ∨ F)		
4.	C ≡ K		
5.	W · (K ∨ L)		
6.	~L	/∴	R
7.	(D ∨ M) · (D ∨ T)	1	Dist
8.	D ∨ M	7	Simp
*9.	S	2,8	MP
10.	K ∨ L	5	Simp
11.	K	10, 6	DS
12.	(C ⊃ K) · (K ⊃ C)	4	MEA
13.	K ⊃ C	12	Simp
14.	C	13,11	MP
15.	~(S ∨ F)	3,14	MP
16.	~S · ~F	15	DeM
*17.	~S	16	Simp
18.	S ∨ R	9	Add
19.	R	18,17	DS

*Valid but not sound; inconsistent premises.

91.	1. F ≡ G		
	2. M ⊃ (W ⊃ S)		
	3. A ⊃ ~G		
	4. M ⊃ W		
	5. (M ⊃ S) ⊃ F	/∴	A ⊃ ~Q
	6. (F ⊃ G) · (G ⊃ F)	1	MEA
	7. F ⊃ G	6	Simp
	8. G ⊃ ~A	3	Transp
	9. F ⊃ ~A	7,8	HS
	10. M ⊃ (M · W)	4	Abs
	11. (M · W) ⊃ S	2	Exp
	12. M ⊃ S	10,11	HS
	13. F	5,12	MP
	14. ~A	9,13	MP
	15. ~A ∨ ~Q	14	Add
	16. A ⊃ ~Q	15	MI

The antecedent of the conclusion is inconsistent with the standing premises. CP would generate an explicit contradiction. Try it.

92. **1. G ≡ (H · T)**
     2. T ≡ S
     3. O ⊃ S   /∴   **(O · H) ⊃ G**
     4. (T ⊃ S) · (S ⊃ T)   2   MEA
     5. S ⊃ T   4   Simp
     6. O ⊃ T   3,5   HS
     7. [G ⊃ (H · T)] · [(H · T) ⊃ G]   1   MEA
     8. (H · T) ⊃ G   7   Simp
     9. (T · H) ⊃ G   8   Com
     10. T ⊃ (H ⊃ G)   9   Exp
     11. O ⊃ (H ⊃ G)   6,10   HS
     12. (O · H) ⊃ G   11   Exp

93. **1. (C ⊃ ~D) · (R ⊃ ~U)**
     2. (C ∨ R) ∨ L   /∴   **~L ⊃ (~~U ⊃ ~D)**
     3. L ∨ (C ∨ R)   2   Com
     4. ~L ⊃ (C ∨ R)   3   MI
     5. C ⊃ ~D   1   Simp
     6. ~C ∨ ~D   5   MI
     7. (~C ∨ ~D) ∨ ~U   6   Add
     8. ~C ∨ (~D ∨ ~U)   7   Assc
     9. R ⊃ ~U   1   Simp
     10. ~R ∨ ~U   9   MI
     11. (~R ∨ ~U) ∨ ~D   10   Add
     12. ~R ∨ (~U ∨ ~D)   11   Assc
     13. ~R ∨ (~D ∨ ~U)   12   Com
     14. [~C ∨ (~D ∨ ~U)] · [~R ∨ (~D ∨ ~U)] 8,13   Conj
     15. [(~D ∨ ~U) ∨ ~C] · [(~D ∨ ~U) ∨ ~R] 14,   Com
     16. (~D ∨ ~U) ∨ (~C · ~R)   15   Dist
     17. (~C · ~R) ∨ (~D ∨ ~U)   16   Com
     18. ~(C ∨ R) ∨ (~D ∨ ~U)   17   DeM
     19. (C ∨ R) ⊃ (~D ∨ ~U)   18   MI

20. ~L ⊃ (~D ∨ ~U)	4,19	HS
21. ~L ⊃ (~U ∨ ~D)	20	Com
22. ~L ⊃ (U ⊃ ~D)	21	MI
23. ~L ⊃ (~~U ⊃ ~D)	22	DN

Such tediousness is worth avoiding. Try the time saving approach shown with the next problem (which has much the same form).

94. **1. (B ⊃ D) · (S ⊃ W)**
     2. (M ∨ S) ∨ B   /∴   **~M ⊃ (~D ⊃ W)**

3. ~M		
4. M ∨ (S ∨ B)	2	Assc
5. S ∨ B	4,3	DS
6. B ∨ S	5	Com
7. D ∨ W	1,6	CD
8. ~D ⊃ W	7	MI
9. ~M ⊃ (~D ⊃ W)	3-8	CP

It could be done the long way, like the previous item.

95. **1. [B ⊃ (M · S)] · (S ⊃ L)**
     2. C ⊃ B
     3. L ⊃ ~I
     4. [(~P · ~I) ⊃ R] · (R ⊃ W)   /∴   **C ⊃ (~P ⊃ W)**

5. C		
6. B	2,5	MP
7. B ⊃ (M · S)	1	Simp
8. M · S	7,6	MP
9. S	8	Simp
10. S ⊃ L	1	Simp
11. L	10,9	MP
12. ~I	3,11	MP
13. ~P		
14. ~P · ~I	13,12	Conj
15. (~P · ~I) ⊃ R	4	Simp
16. R	15,14	MP

17. R ⊃ W	4 Simp
18. W	17,16 MP
19. ~P ⊃ W	13-18 CP
20. C ⊃ (~P ⊃ W)	5-19 CP

You can do it without the nested conditionals using an increasingly familiar pattern (export, commute, export, hypothetical syllogism).

96. 1. ~A ∨ R
    2. ~R
    3. ~A ⊃ ~F
    4. (F ∨ H) ∨ J

5. J ⊃ S	/∴	~S ⊃ H
6. ~S ⊃ ~J	5	Transp
7. J ∨ (F ∨ H)	4	Com
8. ~J ⊃ (F ∨ H)	7	MI
9. ~S ⊃ (F ∨ H)	6,8	HS
10. ~A	1,2	DS
11. ~F	3,10	MP
12. S ∨ (F ∨ H)	9	MI
13. (F ∨ H) ∨ S	12	Com
14. F ∨ (H ∨ S)	13	Assc
15. H ∨ S	14,11	DS
16. S ∨ H	15	Com
17. ~S ⊃ H	16	MI

97. 1. R ≡ O
    2. O ⊃ (R ⊃ S)
    3. (O ⊃ S) ⊃ (W ∨ SS)

4. SB ⊃ ~W	/∴	(O · SB) ⊃ S S
5. (R ⊃ O) · (O ⊃ R)	1	MEA
6. O ⊃ R	5	Simp
7. O ⊃ (O · R)	6	Abs
8. (O · R) ⊃ S	2	Exp
9. O ⊃ S	7,8	HS
10. W ∨ SS	3,9	MP

11. ~W ⊃ SS	10	MI
12. SB ⊃ SS	4,11	HS
13. ~SB ∨ SS	12	MI
14. ~O ∨ (~SB ∨ SS)	13	Add
15. (~O ∨ ~SB) ∨ SS	14	Assc
16. ~(O · SB) ∨ SS	15	DeM
17. (O · SB) ⊃ SS	16	MI

98.   **1. (T · O) · (P ≡ R)**
     2. (B ⊃ S) · (~A ⊃ B)
     3. (S ∨ O) · (~Q ⊃ S)
     4. (S ≡ T) · (P ∨ B)   /∴   **Q ∨ P**

     INVALID: **T O P R B S A Q**
                 T T   F F T T T F

99.   **1. (I ⊃ E) · (B ⊃ T)**
     2. (E · T) ⊃ R
     3. (B ∨ N) · [N ≡ (F · ~F)]   /∴   **I ⊃ (R ≡ T)**

4. I		
5. I ⊃ E	1	Simp
6. E	5,4	MP
7. N ≡ (F · ~F)	3	Simp
8. [N ⊃ (F · ~F)] · [(F · ~F) ⊃ N]	7	MEA
9. N ⊃ (F · ~F)	8	Simp
10. ~N ∨ (F · ~F)	9	MI
11. (~N ∨ F) · (~N ∨ ~F)	10	Dist
12. (N ⊃ F) · (N ⊃ ~F)	11	MI
13. N ⊃ F	12	Simp
14. N ⊃ ~F	12	Simp
15. ~F ⊃ ~N	13	Transp
16. N ⊃ ~N	14,15	HS
17. ~N ∨ ~N	16	MI
18. ~N	17	Taut
19. B ∨ N	3	Simp
20. B	19,18	DS
21. B ⊃ T	1	Simp

22. T	21,20	MP
23. E ⊃ (T ⊃ R)	2	Export
24. T ⊃ R	23,6	MP
25. ~R ∨ T	21	Add
26. R ⊃ T	25	MI
27. (R ⊃ T) · (T ⊃ R)	31,28	Conj
28. R ≡ T	32	MEA
29. I ⊃ (R ≡ T)	4-28	CP

How many shorter ways can you find?

100. 1. (A ∨ B) ⊃ C		
2. ~C ∨ (D · E)		
3. D ⊃ (E ⊃ F)		
4. ~(F ∨ G)		
5. H ≡ ~I		
6. ~G ⊃ (J · I)		
7. (B ∨ H) ∨ K		
8. L ∨ (~K · M)	/∴	L
9. ~F · ~G	4	DeM
10. ~F	9	Simp
11. (D · E) ⊃ F	3	Export
12. ~(D · E)	11,10	MT
13. C ⊃ (D · E)	2	MI
14. ~C	13,12	MT
15. ~(A ∨ B)	1,14	MT
16. ~A · ~B	15	DeM
17. ~B	16	Simp
18. (H ⊃ ~I) · (~I ⊃ H)	5	MEA
19. ~G	9	Simp
20. J · I	6,19	MP
21. I	20	Simp
22. H ⊃ ~I	18	Simp
23. ~~I	21	DN
24. ~H	22,23	MT
25. ~B · ~H	17,24	Conj
26. ~(B ∨ H)	25	DeM

27.	K	7,26	DS
28.	K ∨ ~M	27	Add
29.	~(~K · M)	28	DN
30.	L	8,33	DS

101. 1. **R ≡ (B · F)**
    2. **F ⊃ (B ∨ D)**   /∴   **[(~D · ~W) · F] ⊃ (B · R)**

3.	(~D · ~W) · F		
4.	F	3	Simp
5.	B ∨ D	2,4	MP
6.	~D · (~W · F)	3	Assc
7.	~D	6	Simp
8.	B	5,7	DS
9.	B · F	8,4	Conj
10.	[R ⊃ (B · F)] · [(B · F) ⊃ R]	1	MEA
11.	(B · F) ⊃ R	10	Simp
12.	R	11,9	MP
13.	B · R	8,12	Conj
14.	[(~D · ~W) · F] ⊃ (B · R)	3-13	CP

A straight proof is nearly twice as long.

102. 1. **T ∨ N**
    2. **D ⊃ ~(T · Q)**
    3. **N ⊃ (L ∨ M)**
    4. **Q ∨ ~D**
    5. **L ⊃ ~U**
    6. **M ⊃ F**
    7. **(U ≡ F) ⊃ S**   /∴   **D ⊃ [(F ⊃ U) ⊃ S]**

8.	[(U ⊃ F) · (F ⊃ U)] ⊃ S	7	MEA
9.	(U ⊃ F) ⊃ [(F ⊃ U) ⊃ S]	8	Exp
10.	~D ∨ Q	4	Com
11.	D ⊃ Q	10	MI
12.	D		
13.	Q	11,12	MI
14.	~(T · Q)	2,12	MP

15. ~T ∨ ~Q	14	DeM
16. ~Q ∨ ~T	15	Com
17. Q ⊃ ~T	16	MI
18. ~T	17,13	MP
19. N	1,18	DS
20. L ∨ M	3,19	MP
21. (L ⊃ ~U) · (M ⊃ F)	5,6	Conj
22. ~U ∨ F	21,20	CD
23. U ⊃ F	22	MI
24. (F ⊃ U) ⊃ S	9,23	MP
25. D ⊃ [(F ⊃ U) ⊃ S]	12-24	CP

103.
1. (R ∨ C) ⊃ T		
2. (T ∨ P) ⊃ G		
3. (G ∨ W) ⊃ I		
4. (I ∨ N) ⊃ (D · R)	/∴	**R ≡ G**
5. R		
6. R ∨ C	5	Add
7. T	1,6	MP
8. T ∨ P	7	Add
9. G	2,8	MP
10. R ⊃ G	5-9	CP
11. G		
12. G ∨ W	11	Add
13. I	3,12	MP
14. I ∨ N	13	Add
15. D · R	4,14	MP
16. R	15	Simp
17. G ⊃ R	11-16	CP
18. (R ⊃ G) · (G ⊃ R)	10,17	Conj
19. R ≡ G	18	MEA

Without Conditional Proof, this problem is distinctly tedious.
I do it in just under 40 steps, with repeated distributions and
simplifications. Can you find a shorter route?

104. 1. B ∨ (L · I)
     2. G ⊃ ~B
     3. (L · I) ⊃ ~T   /∴   G ⊃ ~(B ≡ ~T)

     4. G
     5. ~B   2,4   MP
     6. L · I   1,5   DS
     7. ~T   3,6   MP
     8. ~B · ~T   5,7   Conj
     9. ~(B ∨ T)   8   DeM
     10. ~(T ∨ B)   9   Com
     11. ~(~T ⊃ B)   10   MI
     12. ~(~T ⊃ B) ∨ ~(B ⊃ ~T)   11   Add
     13. ~[(~T ⊃ B) · (B ⊃ ~T)]   12   DeM
     14. ~(B ≡ ~T)   13   MEA
     15. B ⊃ ~(B ≡ ~T)   4-14   CP

A straight proof is only slightly longer:

     4. ~B ⊃ (L · I)   1   MI
     5. G ⊃ (L · I)   2,4   HS
     6. G ⊃ ~T   5,3   HS
     7. (G ⊃ ~T) · (G ⊃ ~B)   6,2   Conj
     8. (~G ∨ ~T) · (~G ∨ ~B)   7   MI
     9. ~G ∨ (~T · ~B)   8   Dist
     10. ~G ∨ ~(T ∨ B)   9   DeM
     11. ~G ∨ ~(~T ⊃ B)   10   MI
     12. [~G ∨ ~(~T ⊃ B)] ∨ ~(B ⊃ ~T)   11   Add
     13. ~G ∨ [~(~T ⊃ B) ∨ ~(B ⊃ ~T)]   12   Assc
     14. ~G ∨ ~[(~T ⊃ B) · (B ⊃ ~T)]   13   DeM
     15. ~G ∨ ~[(B ⊃ ~T) · (~T ⊃ B)]   14   Com
     16. ~G ∨ ~(B ≡ ~T)   15   MEA
     17. G ⊃ ~(B ≡ ~T)   19   MI

105. 1. W
     2. (W · S) ⊃ A   /∴   A ≡ A
     3. ~A ∨ W   1   Add
     4. A ⊃ W   3   MI

5. A ⊃ (A · W)	4	Abs
6. ~A ∨ (A · W)	5	MI
7. (~A ∨ A) · (~A ∨ W)	6	Dist
8. ~A ∨ A	7	Simp
9. A ⊃ A	8	MI
10. (A ⊃ A) · (A ⊃ A)	9	taut
11. A ≡ A	10	MEA

Short isn't always easy.

106. **1.**	**~C ⊃ A**		
2.	**S ⊃ C**		
3.	**~S ⊃ ~(C ∨ A)**	/∴	**[(A ⊃ S) ≡ C] ∨ Q**
4.	S ∨ ~(C ∨ A)	3	MI
5.	S ∨ (~C · ~A)	4	DeM
6.	(S ∨ ~C) · (S ∨ ~A)	5	Dist
7.	(S ∨ ~A)	6	Simp
8.	~A ∨ S	7	Com
9.	A ⊃ S	8	MI
10.	A ⊃ C	9,2	HS
11.	~C ⊃ C	1,10	HS
12.	C ∨ C	11	MI
13.	C	12	Taut
14.	(A ⊃ S) · C	9,13	Conj
15.	[(A ⊃ S) · C] ∨ [~(A ⊃ S) · ~C]	14	Add
16.	(A ⊃ S) ≡ C	15	MEB
17.	[(A ⊃ S) ≡ C] ∨ Q	16	Add

Here is an alternative (shorter) route):

4.	(C ∨ A) ⊃ S	3	Transp
5.	C ∨ A	1	MI
6.	S	4,5	MP
7.	C	2,6	MP
8.	~A ∨ S	6	Add
9.	A ⊃ S	8	MI
10.	(A ⊃ S) · C	9,7	Conj

11.	[(A ⊃ S) · C] ∨ [~(A ⊃ S) · ~C]	10	Add
12.	(A ⊃ S) ≡ C	11	MEB
13.	[(A ⊃ S) ≡ C] ∨ Q	12	Add

107. 1.	**D ⊃ (M · Y)**		
2.	**Y ⊃ (J ∨ W)**		
3.	**T ⊃ ~(W ∨ I)**	/∴	**(D · T) ⊃ J**
4.	D · T		
5.	D	4	Simp
6.	M · Y	1,5	MP
7.	Y	6	Simp
8.	J ∨ W	2,7	MP
9.	T	4	Simp
10.	~(W ∨ I)	3,9	MP
11.	~W · ~I	10	DeM
12.	~W	11	Simp
13.	J	8,12	DS
14.	(D · T) ⊃ J	4-13	CP

To run a straight proof, first establish D ⊃ (J ∨ W) as well as T ⊃ ~W. From there it is easy.

108. 1.	**P ⊃ [(L · S) · (M · Y)]**		
2.	**R ⊃ (O · B)**		
3.	**(L · B) ⊃ E**		
4.	**~E · R**	/∴	**~P**
5.	~E	4	Simp
6.	~(L · B)	3,5	MT
7.	~L ∨ ~B	6	DeM
8.	R	4	Simp
9.	O · B	2,8	MP
10.	B	9	Simp
11.	~~B	10	DN
12.	~L	7,11	DS
13.	~L ∨ ~S	12	Add
14.	~(L · S)	13	DeM

15. ~(L · S) ∨ ~(M · Y)	14	Add
16. ~[(L · S) · (M · Y)]	15	DeM
17. ~P	1,16	MT

109.
1. U ≡ I		
2. ~T ⊃ M		
3. P ⊃ D		
4. M ⊃ (D ⊃ I)		
5. (B · L) ⊃ [(~T · P) ∨ U]		
6. (B · L) ∨ G		
7. ~(G ∨ A)	/∴	I
8. ~G · ~A	7	DeM
9. ~G	8	Simp
10. B · L	6,9	DS
11. (~T · P) ∨ U	5,10	MP
12. (U ⊃ I) · (I ⊃ U)	1	MEA
13. U ⊃ I	12	Simp
14. ~T ⊃ (D ⊃ I)	2,4	HS
15. (~T · D) ⊃ I	14	Exp
16. (D · ~T) ⊃ I	15	Com
17. D ⊃ (~T ⊃ I)	16	Exp
18. P ⊃ (~T ⊃ I)	3,17	HS
19. (P · ~T) ⊃ I	18	Exp
20. (~T · P) ⊃ I	19	Com
21. [(~T · P) ⊃ I] · [U ⊃ I]	20,13	Conj
22. I ∨ I	21,11	CD
23. I	22	Taut

If you don't catch the whiff of the potential constructive dilemma, it will take about five more lines.

110.
1. A ⊃ (M · N)		
2. (M · D) ⊃ (H ∨ P)		
3. (H ∨ G) ⊃ C		
4. P ⊃ C	/∴	A ⊃ (D ⊃ C)

5.	A		
6.	M · N	1,5	MP
7.	M	6	Simp
8.	D		
9.	M · D	7,8	Conj
10.	H ∨ P	2,9	MP
11.	H		
12.	H ∨ G	11	Add
13.	C	3,12	MP
14.	H ⊃ C	11-13	CP
15.	(H ⊃ C) · (P ⊃ C)	14,4	Conj
16.	C ∨ C	15,10	CD
17.	C	16	Taut
18.	D ⊃ C	8-17	CP
19.	A ⊃ (D ⊃ C)	5-18	CP

It only takes six more lines to do it without CP; and it is a particularly nice proof:

5.	~A ∨ (M · N)	1	MI
6.	(~A ∨ M) · (~A ∨ N)	5	Dist
7.	~A ∨ M	6	Simp
8.	A ⊃ M	7	MI
9.	M ⊃ [D ⊃ (H ∨ P)]	2	Export
10.	A ⊃ [D ⊃ (H ∨ P)]	8,9	HS
11.	(A · D) ⊃ (H ∨ P)	10	Export
12.	~(H ∨ G) ∨ C	3	MI
13.	(~H · ~G) ∨ C	12	DeM
14.	C ∨ (~H · ~G)	13	Com
15.	(C ∨ ~H) · (C ∨ ~G)	14	Dist
16.	C ∨ ~H	15	Simp
17.	~P ∨ C	4	MI
18.	C ∨ ~P	17	Com
19.	(C ∨ ~H) · (C ∨ ~P)	16,18	Conj
20.	C ∨ (~H · ~P)	19	Dist
21.	C ∨ ~(H ∨ P)	20	DeM
22.	~(H ∨ P) ∨ C	21	Com

23. (H ∨ P) ⊃ C		22	MI
24. (A · D) ⊃ C		11,23	HS
25. A ⊃ (D ⊃ C)		24	Export

111. **1. (B ⊃ ~G) · (R ⊃ O)**
    2. M ≡ S
    3. (M · S) ⊃ (B ∨ R)   /∴   **(M ∨ S) ⊃ (~G ∨ O)**

4. M ∨ S			
5. (M · S) ∨ (~M · ~S)		2	MEB
6. ~(~M · ~S)		4	DeM
7. M · S		5,6	DS
8. B ∨ R		3,7	MP
9. ~G ∨ O		1,8	CD
10. (M ∨ S) ⊃ (~G ∨ O)		4-9	CP

Without CP, note how the manipulation of line one can change it into a conditional (with a hint of Constructive Dilemma).

4. (M · S) ∨ (~M · ~S)		2	MEB
5. (~M · ~S) ∨ (M · S)		4	Com
6. ~(~M · ~S) ⊃ (M · S)		5	MI
7. (M ∨ S) ⊃ (M · S)		6	DeM
8. (M ∨ S) ⊃ (B ∨ R)		7, 3	HS
9. B ⊃ ~G		1	Simp
10. ~B ∨ ~G		9	MI
11. (~B ∨ ~G) ∨ O		10	Add
12. ~B ∨ (~G ∨ O)		11	Assc
13. R ⊃ O		1	Simp
14. ~R ∨ O		13	MI
15. (~R ∨ O) ∨ ~G		14	Add
16. ~R ∨ (O ∨ ~G)		15	Assc
17. ~R ∨ (~G ∨ O)		16	Com
18. [~B ∨ (~G ∨ O)] · [~R ∨ (~G ∨ O)]		12,17	Conj
19. [(~G ∨ O) ∨ ~B] · ((~G ∨ O) ∨ ~R]		18	Com
20. (~G ∨ O) ∨ (~B · ~R)		19	Dist
21. (~B · ~R) ∨ (~G ∨ O)		20	Com

22.	~(B ∨ R) ∨ (~G ∨ O)	21	DeM
23.	(B ∨ R) ⊃ (~G ∨ O)	22	MI
24.	(M ∨ S) ⊃ (~G ∨ O)	3,23	HS

112.
1.	**H ⊃ M**		
2.	**M ⊃ ~P**		
3.	**~P ≡ (~S · R)**	/∴	**H ⊃ (M · R)**
4.	H ⊃ ~P	1,2	HS
5.	[~P ⊃ (~S · R)] · [(~S · R) ⊃ ~P]	3	MEA
6.	~P ⊃ (~S · R)	5	Simp
7.	H ⊃ (~S · R)	4,6	HS
8.	~H ∨ (~S · R)	7	MI
9.	(~H ∨ ~S) · (~H ∨ R)	8	Dist
10.	~H ∨ R	9	Simp
11.	~H ∨ M	1	MI
12.	(~H ∨ M) · (~H ∨ R)	11,10	Conj
13.	~H ∨ (M · R)	12	Dist
14.	H ⊃ (M · R)	13	MI

113.
1.	**Z ∨ (P · C)**		
2.	**G · (B ∨ U)**		
3.	**(Z ∨ P) ⊃ ~F**		
4.	**(G · B) ⊃ F**		
* 5.	**~U**	/∴	**V**
6.	(Z ∨ P) · (Z ∨ C)	1	Dist
7.	Z ∨ P	6	Simp
8.	~F	3,7	MP
9.	~(G · B)	4,8	MT
10.	(G · B) ∨ (G · U)	2	Dist
11.	G · U	10,9	DS
*12.	U	11	Simp
13.	U ∨ V	12	Add
14.	V	13,5	DS

*Valid but not sound; inconsistent premises.

114. **1. M ⊃ B**
   2. (M · B) ⊃ T
   3. M ⊃ (T ⊃ S)
   4. S ⊃ (T ∨ M)
   5. ~(T ∨ S)   /∴   **M ≡ S**
   6. M ⊃ (M · B)   1   Abs
   7. M ⊃ T   6,2   HS
   8. M ⊃ (M · T)   7   Abs
   9. (M · T) ⊃ S   3   Exp
   10. M ⊃ S   8,9   HS
   11. ~T · ~S   5   DeM
   12. ~S   11   Simp
   13. ~S ∨ M   12   Add
   14. S ⊃ M   13   MI
   15. (M ⊃ S) · (S ⊃ M)   10,14 Conj
   16. M ≡ S   15   MEA

Here is another route from line 13:

   13. ~M   12,10 MT
   14. ~M · ~S   13, 12 Conj
   15. (~M · ~S) ∨ (M · S)   14   Add
   16. (M · S) ∨ (~M · ~S)   15   Com
   17. M ≡ S   16   MEB

115. **1. (G ∨ Y) ⊃ (C · T)**
   2. (Y ⊃ T) ⊃ M
   3. (M ≡ F) · ~F   /∴   **P**
   4. M ≡ F   3   Simp
   5. ~F   3   Simp
   6. (M ⊃ F) · (F ⊃ M)   4   MEA
   7. M ⊃ F   6   Simp
   8. ~M   7,5   MT
   9. ~(Y ⊃ T)   2,8   MT
   10. ~(~Y ∨ T)   9   MI
   11. Y · ~T   10   DeM

12.	Y	11	Simp
13.	G ∨ Y	12	Add
14.	C · T	1,13	MP
*15.	~T	11	Simp
*16.	T	14	Simp
17.	T ∨ P	16	Add
18.	P	17,15	DS

*Valid but not sound; inconsistent premises.

116. 1.	**R ∨ (U · W)**		
2.	**~(U ∨ N)**		
3.	**~N ⊃ T**	/∴	**R ≡ T**
4.	~U · ~N	2	DeM
5.	~U	4	Simp
6.	~U ∨ ~W	5	Add
7.	~(U · W)	6	DeM
8.	R	1,7	DS
9.	~N	4	Simp
10.	T	3,9	MP
11.	R · T	8,10	Conj
12.	(R · T) ∨ (~R · ~T)	11	Add
13.	R ≡ T	13	MEB

CP is not very appealing on this one; but here is another way to go at it:

4.	~(R ≡ T)		
5.	~[(R · T) ∨ (~R · ~T)]	4	MEB
6.	~(R · T) · ~(~R · ~T)	5	DeM
7.	~(R · T)	6	Simp
8.	~R ∨ ~T	7	DeM
9.	~T ∨ ~R	8	Com
10.	~U · ~N	2	DeM
11.	~N	10	Simp
12.	T	3,11	MP
13.	T ⊃ ~R	9	MI

14. ~R	13,12	MP
15. U · W	1,14	DS
16. U	15	Simp
17. ~U	10	Simp
18. U · ~U	16,17	Conj
19. R ≡ T	4-18	RAA

117.
1. **(R ∨ S) ⊃ (A ∨ U)**
2. **N ⊃ ~U**
3. **(T ∨ P) ⊃ C**   /∴   **(S · ~C) ⊃ [N ⊃ (A · ~P)]**

4. S		
5. R ∨ S	4	Add
6. A ∨ U	1,5	MP
7. ~C		
8. ~(T ∨ P)	3,7	MT
9. ~T · ~P	8	DeM
10. ~P	9	Simp
11. N		
12. ~U	2,11	MP
13. A	6,12	DS
14. A · ~P	13,10	Conj
15. N ⊃ (A · ~P)	11-14	CP
16. ~C ⊃ [N ⊃ (A · ~P)]	7-15	CP
17. S ⊃ {~C ⊃ [N ⊃ (A · ~P)]}	4-16	CP
18. (S · ~C) ⊃ [N ⊃ (A · ~P)]	17	Export

118.
1. **(H ∨ G) ⊃ [R ∨ (S ∨ K)]**
2. **W ⊃ ~(D ∨ S)**
3. **N ≡ ~K**
4. **T ⊃ (I · N)**   /∴ **~(W · G) ∨ {T ⊃ [R · (~S · ~K)]}**

5. W · G		
6. G	5	Simp
7. H ∨ G	6	Add
8. R ∨ (S ∨ K)	1,7	MP
9. W	5	Simp
10. ~(D ∨ S)	2,9	MP
11. ~D · ~S	10	DeM

12. ~S · ~D	11	Com
13. ~S	12	Simp
14. T		
15. I · N	4,14	MP
16. N	15	Simp
17. (N ⊃ ~K) · (~K ⊃ N)	3	MEA
18. N ⊃ ~K	17	Simp
19. ~K	18,16	MP
20. ~S · ~K	13,19	Conj
21. ~(S ∨ K)	20	DeM
22. R	8,21	DS
23. R · (~S · ~K)	22,20	Conj
24. T ⊃ [R · (~S · ~K)]	14-23	CP
25. (W · G) ⊃ {T ⊃ [R · (~S · ~K)]}	5-24	CP
26. ~(W · G) ∨ {T ⊃ [R · (~S · ~K)]}	25	MI

119. 1. **(E · M) ⊃ [J ⊃ ~(F ∨ L)]**		
2. **~S ⊃ [(C ⊃ J) · (~C ⊃ A)]** /∴ **C ⊃ {~S ⊃ [(M · E) ⊃ ~L]}**		
3. S ∨ [(C ⊃ J) · (~C ⊃ A)]	2	MI
4. [S ∨ (C ⊃ J)] · [S ∨ (~C ⊃ A)]	3	Dist
5. S ∨ (C ⊃ J)	4	Simp
6. ~S ⊃ (C ⊃ J)	5	MI
7. (~S · C) ⊃ J	6	Export
8. (C · ~S) ⊃ J	7	Com
9. [(E · M) · J] ⊃ ~(F ∨ L)	1	Export
10. [J · (E · M)] ⊃ ~(F ∨ L)	9	Com
11. ~[J · (E · M)] ∨ ~(F ∨ L)	10	MI
12. ~[J · (E · M)] ∨ (~F · ~L)	11	DeM
13. {~[J · (E · M)] ∨ ~F} · {~[J · (E · M)] ∨ ~L}	12	Dist
14. ~[J · (E · M)] ∨ ~L	13	Simp
15. [J · (E · M)] ⊃ ~L	14	MI
16. J ⊃ [(E · M) ⊃ ~L]	15	Export
17. J ⊃ [(M · E) ⊃ ~L]	16	Com
18. (C · ~S) ⊃ [(M · E) ⊃ ~L]	8,17	HS
19. C ⊃ {~S ⊃ [(M · E) ⊃ ~L]}	18	Export

120. 1. (K ⊃ D) · (R ⊃ E)
2. (D ∨ E) ⊃ (M ⊃ G)
3. (R · S) ∨ K
4. (K ∨ S) ⊃ (~L ∨ C)   /∴   (M ∨ L) ⊃ (G ∨ C)
5. K ⊃ D   1   Simp
6. ~D ⊃ ~K   5   Transp
7. K ∨ (R · S)   3   Com
8. (K ∨ R) · (K ∨ S)   7   Dist
9. K ∨ R   8   Simp
10. ~K ⊃ R   9   MI
11. ~D ⊃ R   6,10   HS
12. R ⊃ E   1   Simp
13. ~D ⊃ E   11,12   HS
14. D ∨ E   13   MI
15. M ⊃ G   2,14   MP
16. ~M ∨ G   15   MI
17. (~M ∨ G) ∨ C   16   Add
18. ~M ∨ (G ∨ C)   17   Assc
19. K ∨ S   8   Simp
20. ~L ∨ C   4,19   MP
21. (~L ∨ C) ∨ G   20   Add
22. ~L ∨ (C ∨ G)   21   Assc
23. ~L ∨ (G ∨ C)   22   Com
24. [~M ∨ (G ∨ C)] · [~L ∨ (G ∨ C)] 18,23 Conj
25. [(G ∨ C) ∨ ~M] · [(G ∨ C) ∨ ~L] 24   Com
26. (G ∨ C) ∨ (~M · ~L)   25   Dist
27. (~M · ~L) ∨ (G ∨ C)   26   Com
28. ~(M ∨ L) ∨ (G ∨ C)   27   DeM
29. (M ∨ L) ⊃ (G ∨ C)   28   MI

FIVE: PREDICATE SOLUTIONS

1.   **1. (x)(Px ∨ ~Sx)**
     2. Sm   /∴   **Pm**
     3. Pm ∨ ~Sm   1   UI
     4. ~Sm ∨ Pm   3   Com
     5. Sm ⊃ Pm   4   MI
     6. Pm   5,2   MP

2.   **1. Ga · Gs**
     2. (x)(Gx ⊃ Dx)   /∴   **Da**
     3. Ga ⊃ Da   2   UI
     4. Ga   1   Simp
     5. Da   3,4   MP

3.   **1. (x)(Px ⊃ Ex)**
     2. (x)(Ax ⊃ ~Ix)
     3. (x)(Ix ⊃ ~Ex)   /∴   (∃x)(Ax · Px)

INVALID FOR A UNIVERSE OF ONE OR MORE

Pa Ea Aa Ia
 F T F   F

4.   **1. (x)[Lx ∨ (Cx ∨ Ax)]**
     2. (x)[(Cx · ~Rx) ⊃ (Fx · Tx)]   /∴   **(x)[(Tx · ~Ax) ⊃ ~Lx]**

INVALID FOR A UNIVERSE OF ONE OR MORE

La Ca Aa Ra Fa Ta
 T T F F T T

5. 1. (x)(Cx ⊃ Tx)
   2. (x)(Tx ⊃ ~Ax)
   3. (x)(Cx ⊃ Rx)
   4. (∃x)(Fx · Rx)   /∴   (∃x)(Fx · ~Ax)

INVALID FOR A UNIVERSE OF ONE OR MORE

Ca Ta Aa Ra Fa
 F   F   T   T   T

6. 1. (x)(Px ⊃ Bx)
   2. (x)~(Bx · Rx)   /∴   (x)(Rx ⊃ ~Px)
   3. Py ⊃ By   1   UI
   4. ~(By · Ry)   2   UI
   5. ~By ∨ ~Ry   4   DeM
   6. By ⊃ ~Ry   5   MI
   7. Py ⊃ ~Ry   3,6   HS
   8. Ry ⊃ ~Py   7   Transp
   9. (x)(Rx ⊃ ~Px)   8   UG

7. 1. (x)(Rx ⊃ Cs)
   2. (∃x)(Px · Rx)
   3. (∃x)(Cx · Wx)   /∴   (∃x)(Px · Wx)

INVALID FOR A UNIVERSE OF TWO OR MORE

Ra Rb Ca Cb Pa Pb Wa Wb
 T   F   T   T   T   F   F   T

8. 1. (x)[(Lx · Ex) ⊃ Cx]
   2. Lm   /∴   Em ⊃ Cm
   3. (Lm · Em) ⊃ Cm   1   UI
   4. Lm ⊃ (Em ⊃ Cm)   3   Export
   5. Em ⊃ Cm   4,2   MP

9. 1. Sl
   2. Sl ⊃ Gb
   3. (x)(Gx ⊃ Jx)   /∴   (∃x)(Gx · Jx)

4. Gb	1,2	MP
5. Gb ⊃ Jb	3	UI
6. Jb	5,4	MP
7. Gb · Jb	4,6	Conj
8. (∃x)(Gx · Jx)	7	EG

10. **1. (x)[(Mx ∨ Nx) ⊃ (Ex ⊃ Fx))]** /∴ **(x)[(Nx · Fx) ⊃ Ex]**

INVALID FOR A UNIVERSE OF ONE OR MORE

Ma Na Ea Fa
  T   T   F   T

11. **1. (x)[(Bx ∨ Fx) ⊃ Px]**
   2. (x)(Px ⊃ Dx)
   3. Fc /∴ **Dc**

4. (Bc ∨ Fc) ⊃ Pc	1	UI
5. Pc ⊃ Dc	2	UI
6. Bc ∨ Fc	3	Add
7. Pc	4,6	MP
8. Dc	5,7	MP

12. **1. Ck · ~Jk**
   2. Cl · Jl
   3. (x)[(~Cx ∨ ~Jx) ⊃ Bx]
   4. (x)[(Cx · Jx) ⊃ ~Bx] /∴ **Bk · ~Bl**

5. (~Ck ∨ ~Jk) ⊃ Bk	3	UI
6. ~Jk	1	Simp
7. ~Ck ∨ ~Jk	6	Add
8. Bk	5,7	MP
9. (Cl · Jl) ⊃ ~Bl	4	UI
10. ~Bl	9,2	MP
11. Bk · ~Bl	8,10	Conj

13. **1. (x)(Ax ⊃ ~Mx)**
   2. (x)(Gx ⊃ Hx)
   3. (x)(Hx ⊃ Mx)
   4. Gs /∴ **~As**

5.	As ⊃ ~Ms	1	UI
6.	Gs ⊃ Hs	2	UI
7.	Hs ⊃ Ms	3	UI
8.	Hs	6,4	MP
9.	Ms	7,8	MP
10.	~~Ms	9	DN
11.	~As	5,10	MT

14. **1.** **(x)(Nx ⊃ Qx)**
    2. **(∃x)(Vx · Nx)**
    3. **(∃x)(Qx · Fx)**   /∴   **(∃x)(Vx · Fx)**

INVALID FOR A UNIVERSE OF TWO OR MORE:

Na	**Nb**	**Qa**	**Qb**	**Va**	**Vb**	**Fa**	**Fb**
T	F	T	T	T	F	F	T

15. **1.** **(x)[(Fx · Cx) ⊃ (Sx ∨ Bx)]**
    2. **(x)[(Cx · Gx) ⊃ ~Bx]**
    3. **Fm · (Cm · Gm)**   /∴   **Sm**

4.	(Fm · Cm) ⊃ (Sm ∨ Bm)	1	UI
5.	(Cm · Gm) ⊃ ~Bm	2	UI
6.	Fm	3	Simp
7.	Cm · Gm	3	Simp
8.	~Bm	5,7	MP
9.	Cm	7	Simp
10.	Fm · Cm	6,9	Conj
11.	Sm ∨ Bm	4,10	MP
12.	Sm	11,8	DS

16. **1.** **(x)(Mx ∨ Sx)**
    2. **(∃x)(Gx · Rx)**
    3. **(x)(Mx ⊃ Lx)**
    4. **(x)(Rx ⊃ ~Sx)**   /∴   **(∃x)(Mx · Lx)**

5.	Ga · Ra	2	EI
6.	Ma ∨ Sa	1	UI
7.	Ma ⊃ La	3	UI

8.	Ra ⊃ ~Sa	4	UI
9.	Ra	5	Simp
10.	~Sa	8,9	MP
11.	Ma	6,10	D S
12.	La	7,11	MP
13.	Ma · La	11,12	Conj
14.	(∃x)(Mx · Lx)	13	EG

17. 1. (x)[Ax ⊃ (SPx ⊃ ~STx)]
    2. (∃x)[Ax · (SPx · Dx)]
    3. (∃x)[Ax · (STx · Cx)]   /∴   (x)(Dx ⊃ ~Cx)

INVALID FOR A UNIVERSE OF TWO OR MORE

Aa	**Ab**	**SPa**	**SPb**	**STa**	**STb**	**Da**	**Db**	**Ca**	**Cb**
T	T	T	F	F	T	T	T	T	T

18. 1. (x)(Mx ⊃ Px)
    2. (∃x)(Mx · Hx)
    3. (x)(Mx ⊃ Dx)
    4. (∃x)(Dx · ~Px)   /∴   (∃x)(Dx · ~Hx)

VALID FOR A UNIVERSE OF ONE (THE PREMISES ARE INCONSISTENT); BUT INVALID FOR A UNIVERSE OF TWO OR MORE.

Ma	**Mb**	**Pa**	**Pb**	**Ha**	**Hb**	**Da**	**Db**
T	F	T	F	T	T	T	T

19. 1. (∃x)(Fx · Sx)
    2. (∃x)(Fx · Gx)
    3. (x)[(Sx · Gx) ⊃ Ex]   /∴   (∃x)(Fx · Ex)

INVALID FOR A UNIVERSE OF TWO OR MORE

Fa	**Fb**	**Sa**	**Sb**	**Ga**	**Gb**	**Ea**	**Eb**
T	T	T	F	F	T	F	F

20. **1.** **(x)(Ix ∨ Dx)**
     2. **(x)(Cx ⊃ ~Ix)**
     3. **(x)(Gx ⊃ ~Dx)**   /∴   **(x)(Cx ⊃ ~Gx)**
     4. Iy ∨ Dy   1   UI
     5. Cy ⊃ ~Iy   2   UI
     6. Gy ⊃ ~Dy   3   UI
     7. ~Iy ⊃ Dy   4   MI
     8. Cy ⊃ Dy   5,7   HS
     9. Dy ⊃ ~Gy   6   Transp
     10. Cy ⊃ ~Gy   8.9   HS
     11. (x)(Cx ⊃ ~Gx)   10   UG

21. **1.** **(x)(Cx ⊃ Ix)**
     2. **(∃x)(Px · Dx)**
     3. **(x)(Dx ⊃ ~Ix)**   /∴   **(∃x)(Px · ~Cx)**
     4. Pa · Da   2   EI
     5. Da ⊃ ~Ia   3   UI
     6. Da   4   Simp
     7. ~Ia   5,6   MP
     8. Ca ⊃ Ia   1   UI
     9. ~Ca   8,7   MT
     10. Pa   4   Simp
     11. Pa · ~Ca   10,9   Conj
     12. (∃x)(Px · ~Cx)   11   EG

22. **1.** **Gb ∨ Fb**
     2. **(x)(Fx ⊃ ~Wx)**
     3. **(Rb · Yb) · (Wb · Bb)**
     4. **(x)[(Gx ∨ Tx) ⊃ Nx]**
     5. **(x)(Nx ⊃ Ix)**   /∴   **Ib**
     6. Fb ⊃ ~Wb   2   UI
     7. (Gb ∨ Tb) ⊃ Nb   4   UI
     8. Nb ⊃ Ib   5   UI
     9. Wb · Bb   3   Simp
     10. Wb   9   Simp

11. ~~Wb	10	DN
12. ~Fb	6,11	MT
13. Gb	1,12	DS
14. Gb ∨ Tb	13	Add
15. Nb	7,14	MP
16. Ib	8,15	MP

23. **1. (x)[Px ⊃ (Wx · Hx)]**
  2. (x){Px ⊃ [(Wx · Hx) ⊃ Dx]}
  3. (∃x)(Px · ~Dx)   /∴   **(x)[(Kx ∨ Lx) ⊃ Cx]**

4. Pa · ~Da	3	EI
5. Pa ⊃ (Wa · Ha)	1	UI
6. Pa ⊃ [(Wa · Ha) ⊃ Da]	2	UI
7. Pa	4	Simp
8. Wa · Ha	5,7	MP
9. (Wa · Ha) ⊃ Da	6,7	MP
*10. Da	9,8	MP
*11. ~Da	4	Simp
12. Da ∨ (x)[(Kx ∨ Lx) ⊃ Cx]	10	Add
13. (x)[(Kx ∨ Lx) ⊃ Cx]	12,11	DS

*VALID BUT UNSOUND; INCONSISTANT PREMISES.

24. **1. (x)[(Wx ∨ Gx) ⊃ (Fx · Dx)]** /∴   **(x)(Gx ⊃ Dx)**

2. (Wy ∨ Gy) ⊃ (Fy · Dy)	1	UI
3. Gy		
4. Wy ∨ Gy	3	Add
5. Fy · Dy	2,4	MP
6. Dy	5	Simp
7. Gy ⊃ Dy	3-6	CP
8. (x)(Gx ⊃ Dx)	7	UG

25. **1. (x)(Bx ⊃ Fx)**   /∴ **(x)[(Bx · Px) ⊃ (Bx · Fx)]**

2. By ⊃ Fy	1	UI
3. By ⊃ (By · Fy)	2	abs

4. By · Py		
5. By	4	Simp
6. By · Fy	3,5	MP
7. (By · Py) ⊃ (By · Fy)	4-6	CP
8. (x)[(Bx · Px) ⊃ (Bx · Fx)]	7	UG

26. **1. (x)[(Mx ∨ Jx) ⊃ Ex]**
    2. (x)[(Ex ∨ Rx) ⊃ Bx]   /∴   **(x)(Jx ⊃ Bx)**

3. (My ∨ Jy) ⊃ Ey	1	UI
4. (Ey ∨ Ry) ⊃ By	2	UI
5. Jy		
6. My ∨ Jy	5	Add
7. Ey	3,6	MP
8. Ey ∨ Ry	7	Add
9. By	4,8	MP
10. Jy ⊃ By	5-9	CP
11. (x)(Jx ⊃ Bx)	10	UG

27. **1. (x)(Px ⊃ Mx)**
    2. (x)(~Vx ⊃ ~Px)
    3. (x)[(Mx · Vx) ⊃ ~Ax]   /∴   **Pg ⊃ ~Ag**

4. Pg ⊃ Mg	1	UI
5. ~Vg ⊃ ~Pg	2	UI
6. (Mg · Vg) ⊃ ~Ag	3	UI
7. Pg		
8. Mg	4,7	MP
9. Pg ⊃ Vg	5	Transp
10. Vg	9,7	MP
11. Mg · Vg	8,10	Conj
12. ~Ag	6,11	MP
13. Pg ⊃ ~Ag	7-12	CP

It is actually one line shorter without CP:

7. Pg ⊃ Vg	5	Transp
8. (Pg ⊃ Mg) · (Pg ⊃ Vg)	4,7	Conj
9. (~Pg ∨ Mg) · (~Pg ∨ Vg)	8	MI

10. ~Pg ∨ (Mg · Vg)	9	Dist
11. Pg ⊃ (Mg · Vg)	10	MI
12. Pg ⊃ ~Ag	11,6	H S

28 **1. (x)[(Mx ∨ Qx) ⊃ (Rx · Sx)]**

    2. (x)[(Sx · Ex) ⊃ Tx]   /∴ **(x)[(Qx · Ex) ⊃ (Tx ∨ Wx)]**

3. (My ∨ Qy) ⊃ (Ry · Sy)	1	UI
4. (Sy · Ey) ⊃ Ty	2	UI
5. Qy · Ey		
6. Qy	5	Simp
7. My ∨ Qy	6	Add
8. Ry · Sy	3,7	MP
9. Sy	8	Simp
10. Ey	5	Simp
11. Sy · Ey	9,10	Conj
12. Ty	4,11	MP
13. Ty ∨ Wy	12	Add
14. (Qy · Ey) ⊃ (Ty ∨ Wy)	5-13	CP
15. (x)[(Qx · Ex) ⊃ (Tx ∨ Wx)]	14	UG

29. **1. (x){[(Ax ∨ Ox) ∨ (Dx ∨ Fx)] ⊃ [Gx · (Tx · Cx)]}**

                         /∴   **(x)(Fx ⊃ Tx)**

2. [(Ay ∨ Oy) ∨ (Dy ∨ Fy)] ⊃ [Gy · (Ty · Cy)]	1	UI
3. Fy		
4. [(Ay ∨ Oy) ∨ Dy] ∨ Fy	3	Add
5. (Ay ∨ Oy) ∨ (Dy ∨ Fy)	4	Assc
6. Gy · (Ty · Cy)	2,5	MP
7. Ty · Cy	6	Simp
8. Ty	7	Simp
9. Fy ⊃ Ty	3-8	CP
10. (x)(Fx ⊃ Tx)	9	UG

30. **1. (x)(Sx ⊃ Dx)**

    2. (x)(Dx ⊃ ~Ex) /∴ **(x)[{Sx · [Jx · (Fx · (Gx · Tx))]} ⊃ ~Ex]**

3. Sy ⊃ Dy	1	UI
4. Dy ⊃ ~Ey	2	UI

5. Sy · [Jy · (Fy · (Gy · Ty))]		
6. Sy	3	Simp
7. Sy ⊃ ~Ey	3,4	HS
8. ~Ey	7,6	MP
9. {Sy · [Jy · (Fy · (Gy · Ty))]} ⊃ ~Ey	5-9	CP
10. (x)[{Sx · [Jx · (Fx · (Gx · Tx))]} ⊃ ~Ex]	9	UG

Note: Ex = x is eaten by Real Men.

31. 1. **(x)[(Px ∨ Gx) ⊃ (Jx · Tx)]**
    2. **(x)(~Tx ∨ Ax)**   /∴   **(x)(Px ⊃ Ax)**
    3. (Py ∨ Gy) ⊃ (Jy · Ty)   1   UI
    4. ~Ty ∨ Ay   2   UI
    5. Py
    6. Py ∨ Gy   5   Add
    7. Jy · Ty   3,6   MP
    8. Ty   7   Simp
    9. Ty ⊃ Ay   4   MI
    10. Ay   9,8   MP
    11. Py ⊃ Ay   5-10   CP
    12. (x)(Px ⊃ Ax)   11   UG

32. 1. **(x)[(Lx ∨ Rx) ⊃ (Ox · Ex)]**
    2. **(x)[(Ex ∨ Hx) ⊃ (Ix · Nx)]**   /∴   **(x)(Rx ⊃ Ix)**
    3. (Ly ∨ Ry) ⊃ (Oy · Ey)   1   UI
    4. (Ey ∨ Hy) ⊃ (Iy · Ny)   2   UI
    5. Ry
    6. Ly ∨ Ry   5   Add
    7. Oy · Ey   3,6   MP
    8. Ey   7   Simp
    9. Ey ∨ Hy   8   Add
    10. Iy · Ny   4,9   MP
    11. Iy   10   Simp
    12. Ry ⊃ Iy   5-11   CP
    13. (x)(Rx ⊃ Ix)   12   UG

33.　1. (x)[(Cx ∨ Fx) ⊃ (Ix · Px)]
　　2. (x)[(Ix ∨ Zx) ⊃ (Dx · ~Tx)]　　/∴　(x)(Cx ⊃ ~T)
　　3. (Cy ∨ Fy) ⊃ (Iy · Py)　　　　1　UI
　　4. (Iy ∨ Zy) ⊃ (Dy · ~Ty)　　　2　UI
　　5. Cy
　　6. Cy ∨ Fy　　　　　　　　　　5　Add
　　7. Iy · Py　　　　　　　　　　3,6　MP
　　8. Iy　　　　　　　　　　　　7　Simp
　　9. Iy ∨ Zy　　　　　　　　　　8　Add
　　10. Dy · ~Ty　　　　　　　　　4,9　MP
　　11. ~Ty　　　　　　　　　　　10　Simp
　　12. Cy ⊃ ~Ty　　　　　　　　5-11　CP
　　13. (x)(Cx ⊃ ~Tx)　　　　　　12　UG

34.　1. (x)[(Rx ∨ Sx) ⊃ Cx]
　　2. (x)[(Cx ∨ Mx) ⊃ (Ax ∨ Hx)]
　　3. (x)(Rx ⊃ ~Ax)　　　　　　/∴　(x)(Rx ⊃ Hx)
　　4. (Ry ∨ Sy) ⊃ Cy　　　　　　1　UI
　　5. (Cy ∨ My) ⊃ (Ay ∨ Hy)　　2　UI
　　6. Ry ⊃ ~Ay　　　　　　　　3　UI
　　7. Ry
　　8. Ry ∨ Sy　　　　　　　　　7　Add
　　9. Cy　　　　　　　　　　　　4,8　MP
　　10. Cy ∨ My　　　　　　　　　9　Add
　　11. Ay ∨ Hy　　　　　　　　　5,10　MP
　　12. ~Ay　　　　　　　　　　　6,7　MP
　　13. Hy　　　　　　　　　　　11,12 DS
　　14. Ry ⊃ Hy　　　　　　　　7-13　CP
　　15. (x)(Rx ⊃ Hx)　　　　　　14　UG

35.　1. (x)[(Mx ∨ Nx) ⊃ (Ax · Ex)]
　　2. (x)[(Ax ∨ Cx) ⊃ ~(Tx ∨ Px)]　　/∴　(x)(Nx ⊃ ~Px)
　　3. (My ∨ Ny) ⊃ (Ay · Ey)　　1　UI
　　4. (Ay ∨ Cy) ⊃ ~(Ty ∨ Py)　2　UI
　　5. ~(My ∨ Ny) ∨ (Ay · Ey)　3　MI
　　6. [~(My ∨ Ny) ∨ Ay] · [~(My ∨ Ny) ∨ Ey]　5　Dist

7. ~(My ∨ Ny) ∨ Ay	6	Simp	
8. [~(My ∨ Ny) ∨ Ay] ∨ Cy	7	Add	
9. ~(My ∨ Ny) ∨ (Ay ∨ Cy)	8	Assc	
10. (My ∨ Ny) ⊃ (Ay ∨ Cy)	9	MI	
11. (My ∨ Ny) ⊃ ~(Ty ∨ Py)	10,4	HS	
12. ~(My ∨ Ny) ∨ ~(Ty ∨ Py)	11	MI	
13. (~My · ~Ny) ∨ (~Ty · ~Py)	12	DeM	
14. [(~My · ~Ny) ∨ ~Ty] · [(~My · ~Ny) ∨ ~Py]	13	Dist	
15. (~My · ~Ny) ∨ ~Py	14	Simp	
16. ~Py ∨ (~My · ~Ny)	15	Com	
17. (~Py ∨ ~My) · (~Py ∨ ~Ny)	16	Dist	
18. ~Py ∨ ~Ny	17	Simp	
19. ~Ny ∨ ~Py	18	Com	
20. Ny ⊃ ~Py	19	MI	
21. (x)(Nx ⊃ ~Px)	20	UG	

For good practice in manipulating the apparatus, it is useful to eschew conditional proof from time to time.

36. **1. (x)[Nx ⊃ (Ax · Fx)]**
    2. (∃x)[(Ax · Bx) · Cx)]
    3. (x)[(Ax · Cx) ⊃ ~(Fx ∨ Rx)]   /∴   **(x)[(Nx · Ax) ⊃ ~Bx]**

INVALID FOR A UNIVERSE OF TWO OR MORE

Na	Nb	Aa	Ab	Fa	Fb	Ba	Bb	Ca	Cb	Ra	Rb
T	F	T	T	T	F	T	T	F	T	T	F

37. **1. (x)[(Ax · Mx) ⊃ (~Px ∨ Rx)]**
    2. (∃x)(~Rx · Bx)   /∴   **(∃x){~Bx ⊃ [~(Ax · Mx) ∨ ~Rx)]}**

3. ~Ra · Ba	2	EI
4. Ba	3	Simp
5. Ba ∨ [~(Aa · Ma) ∨ ~Ra)]	4	Add
6. ~Ba ⊃ [~(Aa · Ma) ∨ ~Ra)]	5	MI
7. (∃x){~Bx ⊃ [~(Ax · Mx) ∨ ~Rx)]}	6	EG

The first premise is completely irrelevant here. Note also that the conditions under which an existential conditional would be false are extremely rare. (A vacant universe, or one in which every individual satisfies the antecedent but not the consequent, would be necessary).

38. 1. **(x)[Ax ⊃ (Tx ⊃ Bx)]**
    /∴ **(x)|[(Ax · Tx) · (Sx · Rx)] ⊃ [(Bx ∨ Ex) ∨ (Mx ∨ Dx)]**

2. Ay ⊃ (Ty ⊃ By)	1	UI
3. (Ay · Ty) ⊃ By	2	Export
4. (Ay · Ty) · (Sy · Ry)		
5. Ay · Ty	4	Simp
6. By	3,5	MP
7. By ∨ [Ey ∨ (My ∨ Dy)]	6	Add
8. (By ∨ Ey) ∨ (My ∨ Dy)	7	Assc
9. [(Ay · Ty) · (Sy · Ry)] ⊃ [(By ∨ Ey) ∨ (My ∨ Dy)]	4-8	CP
10. (x){[(Ax · Tx) · (Sx · Rx)] ⊃ [(Bx ∨ Ex) ∨ (Mx ∨ Dx)]}	9	UG

39. 1. **(x){[(Lx ∨ Ax) ∨ (Cx ∨ Mx)] ⊃ [Dx · (Px · Sx)]}**
    /∴ **(x)(Mx ⊃ Sx)**

2. [(Ly ∨ Ay) ∨ (Cy ∨ My)] ⊃ [Dy · (Py · Sy)]	1	UI
3. My		
4. [(Ly ∨ Ay) ∨ Cy] ∨ My	3	Add
5. (Ly ∨ Ay) ∨ (Cy ∨ My)	4	Assc
6. Dy · (Py · Sy)	2,5	MP
7. (Dy · Py) · Sy	6	Assc
8. Sy	7	Simp
9. My ⊃ Sy	3-8	CP
10. (x)(Mx ⊃ Sx)	9	UG

40. **RESTRICTED DOMAIN.** Let x = U.R. dean.

1. **(x)(Px ∨ Tx)**		
2. **(x)(Tx ⊃ ~Px)** /∴ **(x)[(~Tx · Px) ∨ (Tx · ~Px)]**		
3. Py ∨ Ty	1	UI
4. Ty ⊃ ~Py	2	UI
5. ~Py ⊃ Ty	3	MI
6. (Ty ⊃ ~Py) · (~Py ⊃ Ty)	4,5	Conj
7. Ty ≡ ~Py	6	MEA

8.	(Ty · ~Py) ∨ (~Ty · ~~Py)	7	MEB
9.	(Ty · ~Py) ∨ (~Ty · Py)	8	DN
10.	(~Ty · Py) ∨ (Ty · ~Py)	9	Com
11.	(x)[(~Tx · Px) ∨ (Tx · ~Px)]	10	UG

41. 1.	**(x)[(Sx · Tx) ∨ ~Rx]**		
2.	**(x)[(Tx · ~Sx) ⊃ (Mx ∨ Dx)]** /∴	**(x)[(Dx · Rx) ⊃ Tx]**	
3.	(Sy · Ty) ∨ ~Ry	1	UI
4.	~Ry ∨ (Sy · Ty)	3	Com
5.	(~Ry ∨ Sy) · (~Ry ∨ Ty)	4	Dist
6.	~Ry ∨ Ty	5	Simp
7.	~Dy ∨ (~Ry ∨ Ty)	6	Add
8.	(~Dy ∨ ~Ry) ∨ Ty	7	Assc
9.	~(Dy · 'Ry) ∨ Ty	8	DeM
10.	(Dy · Ry) ⊃ Ty	9	MI
11.	(x)[(Dx · Rx) ⊃ Tx]	10	UG

The second premise does not contribute to the argument. Arguments in the real world are often padded (like term papers).

42. 1.	**(x)(Px ⊃ ~Hx)**		
2.	**(x)(~Px ⊃ Nx)**		
3.	**(x)[Qx ⊃ (Hx · ~Nx)]**	/∴	**(x)~Qx**
4.	Py ⊃ ~Hy	1	UI
5.	~Py ⊃ Ny	2	UI
6.	Qy ⊃ (Hy · ~Ny)	3	UI
7.	Hy ⊃ ~Py	4	Transp
8.	Hy ⊃ Ny	7,5	HS
9.	~Hy ∨ Ny	8	MI
10.	~(Hy · ~Ny)	9	DeM
11.	~Qy	6,10	MT
12.	(x)~Qx	11	UG

43. 1.	**(∃x)(Tx · ~Px)**		
2.	**(∃x)(Tx · Px)**		
3.	**(x)[(Tx · Px) ⊃ Cx]**		
4.	**(x)(Cx ≡ Zx)**	/∴	**(∃x)[(Tx · Px) · Zx]**

5. Ta · Pa	2	EI
6. (Ta · Pa) ⊃ Ca	3	UI
7. Ca ≡ Za	4	UI
8. Ca	6,5	MP
9. (Ca ⊃ Za) · (Za ⊃ Ca)	8	MEA
10. Ca ⊃ Za	9	Simp
11. Za	10,8	MP
12. (Ta · Pa) · Za	5,11	Conj
13. (∃x)[(Tx · Px) · Zx]	12	EG

44.
1. **(x)[(Cx · ~Tx) ⊃ Mx]**		
2. **(x)(Gx ⊃ Cx)**		
3. **(∃x)(Gx · ~Mx)**	/∴	**(∃x)Tx**
4. Ga · ~Ma	3	EI
5. (Ca · ~Ta) ⊃ Ma	1	UI
6. Ga ⊃ Ca	2	UI
7. Ga	4	Simp
8. Ca	6,7	MP
9. ~Ma	4	Simp
10. ~(Ca · ~Ta)	5,9	MT
11. ~Ca ∨ Ta	10	DeM
12. Ca ⊃ Ta	11	MI
13. Ta	12,8	MP
14. (∃x)Tx	13	EG

45.
1. **(x)[(Fx ∨ Sx) ⊃ (Ux · Nx)]**		
2. **(x)[(Ux ∨ ~Ex) ⊃ ~(Ax ∨ Vx)]**	/∴	**(x)(Fx ⊃ ~Vx)**
3. (Fy ∨ Sy) ⊃ (Uy · Ny)	1	UI
4. (Uy ∨ ~Ey) ⊃ ~(Ay ∨ Vy)	2	UI
⎡ 5. Fy		
⎢ 6. Fy ∨ Sy	5	Add
⎢ 7. Uy · Ny	3,6	MP
⎢ 8. Uy	7	Simp
⎢ 9. Uy ∨ ~Ey	8	Add
⎢ 10. ~(Ay ∨ Vy)	4,9	MP
⎣ 11. ~Ay · ~Vy	10	DeM

	12. ~Vy	11	Simp
	13. Fy ⊃ ~Vy	5-12	CP
	14. (x)(Fx ⊃ ~Vx)	13	UG

46. 1. **(x)[(Mx · Fx) ⊃ Ax]**
  2. **(x)(Sx ⊃ Mx)**
  3. **(x)(Ex ⊃ Fx)**
  4. **(∃x)Ax**   /∴   **(∃x)(Sx · Ex)**

INVALID FOR A UNIVERSE OF ONE OR MORE

Ma Fa Aa Sa Ea
  T   T   T   F   F

47. 1. **(x)[Ax ⊃ (Mx · Fx)]**
  2. **(x)(Mx ⊃ Sx)**
  3. **(x)(Fx ⊃ Ex)**
  4. **(∃x)Ax**   /∴   **(∃x)(Sx · Ex)**

5. Aa	4	EI
6. Aa ⊃ (Ma · Fa)	1	UI
7. Ma ⊃ Sa	2	UI
8. Fa ⊃ Ea	3	UI
9. Ma · Fa	6,5	MP
10. Ma	9	Simp
11. Fa	9	Simp
12. Sa	7,10	MP
13. Ea	8,11	MP
14. Sa · Ea	12,13	Conj
15. (∃x)(Sx · Ex)	14	EG

48. 1. **(x)(Fx ≡ Gx)**
  2. **(x)(Fx ⊃ Dx)**
  3. **(x)(Hx ⊃ Gx)**
  4. **(x)[(Hx · Dx) ⊃ ~Sx]**   /∴   **(x)(Hx ⊃ ~Sx)**

5. Fy ≡ Gy	1	UI
6. Fy ⊃ Dy	2	UI
7. Hy ⊃ Gy	3	UI

8. (Hy · Dy) ⊃ ~Sy	4	UI
9. (Fy ⊃ Gy) · (Gy ⊃ Fy)	5	MEA
10. Gy ⊃ Fy	9	Simp
11. Hy ⊃ Fy	7,10	HS
12. Hy ⊃ Dy	11,6	HS
13. Hy ⊃ (Hy · Dy)	12	Abs
14. Hy ⊃ ~Sy	13,8	HS
15. (x)(Hx ⊃ ~Sx)	14	UG

49. **1. (x)(~Hx ⊃ ~Tx)**
    2. (x)(~Tx ⊃ Bx)
    3. (∃x)(Lx · Ix)
    4 ~(x)(Ix ⊃ Hx)   /∴   **(∃x)(Lx · Bx)**

INVALID FOR A UNIVERSE OF TWO OR MORE:

Ha	Hb	Ta	Tb	Ba	Bb	La	Lb	Ia	Ib
T	F	T	F	F	T	T	F	T	T

50. **1. (∃x)(Mx · Ox)**
    2. (x)Mx ⊃ Rx
    3. (x)[(Px · Rx) ⊃ Sx]
    4. (x)(Ox ⊃ Px)   /∴   **(∃x)(Mx · Sx)**

5. Ma · Oa	1	EI
6. Ma ⊃ Ra	2	UI
7. (Pa · Ra) ⊃ Sa	3	UI
8. Oa ⊃ Pa	4	UI
9. Oa	5	Simp
10. Pa	8,9	MP
11. Ma	5	Simp
12. Ra	6,11	MP
13. Pa · Ra	10,12	Conj
14. Sa	7,13	MP
15. Ma · Sa	11,14	Conj
16. (∃x)(Mx · Sx)	15	EG

51. **1.** **(x)[Tx ⊃ (Px ⊃ Fx)]**
    2. **(x)[(Ax · Cx) ⊃ Rx]**
    3. **(x)[(Rx · Fx) ⊃ Kx]**   **/∴ (x){[(Ax · Cx) · (Tx · Px)] ⊃ Kx}**

4. Ty ⊃ (Py ⊃ Fy)	1	UI
5. (Ay · Cy) ⊃ Ry	2	UI
6. (Ry · Fy) ⊃ Ky	3	UI
7. (Ay · Cy) · (Ty · Py)		
8. Ay · Cy	7	Simp
9. Ry	5,8	MP
10. Ty · Py	7	Simp
11. (Ty · Py) ⊃ Fy	4	Export
12. Fy	11,10	MP
13. Ry · Fy	9,12	Conj
14. Ky	6,13	MP
15. [(Ay · Cy) · (Ty · Py)] ⊃ Ky	7-14	CP
16. (x){[(Ax · Cx) · (Tx · Px)] ⊃ Kx}	15	UG

52. **1.** **(x)[(Cx · Hx) ⊃ Px]**
    2. **(x)[~Hx ⊃ (Sx · Nx)]**
    3. **(∃x)(Cs · Sx)**
    4. **(x)(Cx ⊃ ~Nx)**   **/∴   (x)(Cx ⊃ Px)**

5. (Cy · Hy) ⊃ Py	1	UI
6. ~Hy ⊃ (Sy · Ny)	2	UI
7. Cy ⊃ ~Ny	4	UI
8. Cy		
9. ~Ny	7,8	MP
10. ~Sy ∨ ~Ny	9	Add
11. ~(Sy · Ny)	10	DeM
12. Hy	6,11	MT
13. Cy · Hy	8,12	Conj
14. Py	5,13	MP
15. Cy ⊃ Py	8-14	CP
16. (x)(Cx ⊃ Px)	15	UG

The fact that some in the class were sophomores is beside the point. The universal conclusion is supported by the other premises. So no existential fallacy occurs.

53.   **1. (x)[(Lx ∨ Cx) ⊃ Mx]**
    2. (x)[(Dx · Mx) ⊃ Ex]   /∴   **(x)[(Dx · Lx) ⊃ Ex]**
    3. (Ly ∨ Cy) ⊃ My   1   UI
    4. (Dy · My) ⊃ Ey   2   UI
    5. (My · Dy) ⊃ Ey   4   Com
    6. My ⊃ (Dy ⊃ Ey)   5   Export
    7. (Ly ∨ Cy) ⊃ (Dy ⊃ Ey)   3,6   HS
    8. ~(Ly ∨ Cy) ∨ (Dy ⊃ Ey)   7   MI
    9. (~Ly · ~Cy) ∨ (Dy ⊃ Ey)   8   DeM
   10. (Dy ⊃ Ey) ∨ (~Ly · ~Cy)   9   Com
   11. [(Dy ⊃ Ey) ∨ ~Ly] · [(Dy ⊃ Ey) ∨ ~Cy] 10   Dist
   12. (Dy ⊃ Ey) ∨ ~Ly   11   Simp
   13. ~Ly ∨ (Dy ⊃ Ey)   12   Com
   14. Ly ⊃ (Dy ⊃ Ey)   13   MI
   15. (Ly · Dy) ⊃ Ey   14   Export
   16. (Dy · Ly) ⊃ Ey   15   Com
   17. (x)[(Dx · Lx) ⊃ Ex]   16   UG

54.   **1. ~(x)(Rx ⊃ Lx)**
    2. (x)[Rx ⊃ (Ox ⊃ Lx)]
    3. (x)[(Ox ⊃ ~Ix) · (~Ox ⊃ Ix)] /∴   **(∃x)(Rx · Ix)**
    4. (∃x)~(Rx ⊃ Lx)   1   QN
    5. ~(Ra ⊃ La)   4   EI
    6. ~(~Ra ∨ La)   5   MI
    7. Ra · ~La   6   DeM
    8. Ra ⊃ (Oa ⊃ La)   2   UI
    9. (Oa ⊃ ~Ia) · (~Oa ⊃ Ia)   3   UI
   10. Ra   7   Simp
   11. Oa ⊃ La   8,10   MP
   12. ~La   7   Simp
   13. ~Oa   11,12 MT
   14. ~Oa ⊃ Ia   9   Simp
   15. Ia   14,13 MP
   16. Ra · Ia   10,15 Conj
   17. (∃x)(Rx · Ix)   16   EG

55. 1. (x)(Ux ⊃ Bx)
    2. ~Bf
    3. (x)(~Ux ⊃ Tx)
    4. (x)[Tx ≡ (Vx ∨ Ox)]
    5. ~Vf
    6. Of ⊃ (Pf · Nf)   /∴   Nf
    7. Uf ⊃ Bf   1   UI
    8. ~Uf   7,2   MT
    9. ~Uf ⊃ Tf   3   UI
   10. Tf   9,8   MP
   11. Tf ≡ (Vf ∨ Of)   4   UI
   12. [Tf ⊃ (Vf ∨ Of)] · [(Vf ∨ Of) ⊃ Tf]   11   MEA
   13. Tf ⊃ (Vf ∨ Of)   12   Simp
   14. Vf ∨ Of   13,10   MP
   15. Of   14,5   DS
   16. Pf · Nf   6,15   MP
   17. Nf   16   Simp

56. 1. (x)[(Sx ∨ Lx) ⊃ Rx]
    2. (X)[(Rx ∨ Bx) ⊃ Ox]   /∴   (x)(Sx ⊃ Ox)
    3. ~(x)(Sx ⊃ Ox)
    4. (∃x)~(Sx ⊃ Ox)   3   QN
    5. ~(Sa ⊃ Oa)   4   EI
    6. ~(~Sa ∨ Oa)   5   MI
    7. Sa · ~Oa   6   DeM
    8. Sa   7   Simp
    9. (Sa ∨ La) ⊃ Ra   1   UI
   10. Sa ∨ La   8   Add
   11. Ra   9,10   MP
   12. (Ra ∨ Ba) ⊃ Oa   2   UI
   13. Ra ∨ Ba   11   Add
   14. Oa   12,13   MP
   15. ~Oa   7   Simp
   16. Oa · ~Oa   14,15   Conj
   17. (x)(Sx ⊃ Ox)   3-16   RAA

57.   1. (x){Hx ⊃ [(Mx ∨ Fx) ⊃ Dx]}
     2. (Ms · Hs) · (Fz · Hz)   /∴   ~(~Ds ∨ ~Dz)
     3. Ms · Hs   2   Simp
     4. Hs ⊃ [(Ms ∨ Fs) ⊃ Ds]   1   UI
     5. Hs   3   Simp
     6. (Ms ∨ Fs) ⊃ Ds   4,5   MP
     7. Ms   3   Simp
     8. Ms ∨ Fs   7   Add
     9. Ds   6,8   MP
   10. Hz ⊃ [(Mz ∨ Fz) ⊃ Dz]   1   UI
   11. Fz · Hz   2   Simp
   12. Hz   11   Simp
   13. (Mz ∨ Fz) ⊃ Dz   10,12 MP
   14. Fz   11   Simp
   15. Mz ∨ Fz   14   Add
   16. Dz   13,15 MP
   17. Ds · Dz   9,16   Add
   18. ~(~Ds ∨ ~Dz)   17   DeM

58. **RESTRICTED DOMAIN:** x = Lotus.
     1. (x)[Px ⊃ (Wx ⊃ ~Tx)]
     2. (x)(Ex ⊃ Px)
     3. (x)[(Px · ~Tx) ⊃ Fx]
     4. (x)(Fx ⊃ Wx)   /∴   (x)[Ex ⊃ (Fx ≡ Wx)]
     5. Py ⊃ (Wy ⊃ ~Ty)   1   UI
     6. Ey ⊃ Py   2   UI
     7. (Py · ~Ty) ⊃ Fy   3   UI
     8. Fy ⊃ Wy   4   UI
     9. Ey
   10. Py   6,9   MP
   11. Wy ⊃ ~Ty   5,10   MP
   12. Py ⊃ (~Ty ⊃ Fy)   7   Export
   13. ~Ty ⊃ Fy   12.10 MP
   14. Wy ⊃ Fy   11,13   HS
   15. (Fy ⊃ Wy) · (Wy ⊃ Fy)   8,14   Conj
   16. Fy ≡ Wy   15   MEA

17. Ey ⊃ (Fy ≡ Wy)   9-16   CP
18. (x)[Ex ⊃ (Fx ≡ Wx)]   17   UG

59. 1. (∃x)[Ux · (Fx ∨ Sx)]
     2. (∃x)[Ux · (Px · Hx)]
     3. (x){[Fx · (Px · Hx)] ⊃ Gx}   /∴   (∃x)(Ux · Gx)
INVALID FOR A UNIVERSE OF TWO OR MORE
Ua Ub Fa Fb Sa Sb Pa Pb Ha Hb Ga Gb
 T   T   T   F   F   F   F   F   T   F   T   F

60. 1. (∃x)Mx
     2. (x)[Mx ⊃ (Lx · Cx)]
     3. (x)(Cx ⊃ Sx)
     4. (x){[(Lx · Cx) · Sx] ⊃ Dx}
     5. (x)(Mx ⊃ Ex)   /∴   (∃x)(Ex · Dx)
     6. Ma   1   EI
     7. Ma ⊃ (La · Ca)   2   UI
     8. Ca ⊃ Sa   3   UI
     9. [(La · Ca) · Sa] ⊃ Da   4   UI
    10. Ma ⊃ Ea   5   UI
    11. Ea   10,6   MP
    12. La · Ca   7,6   MP
    13. Ca   12   Simp
    14. Sa   8,13   MP
    15. (La · Ca) · Sa   12,14 Conj
    16. Da   9,15   MP
    17. Ea · Da   11,16 Conj
    18. (∃x)(Ex · Dx)   17   EG

61. 1. (x)[(Cx ⊃ ~Ax) · (Lx ⊃ ~Rx)]
     2. (x)[(~Ax ∨ ~Rx) ⊃ Wx]
     3. (x)[(Wx ∨ ~Ex) ⊃ ~Sx]
     4. (x)[(Px · Mx) ⊃ Lx]   /∴   (x)[(Px · Mx) ⊃ ~Sx]
     5. (Cy ⊃ ~Ay) · (Ly ⊃ ~Ry)   1   UI
     6. (~Ay ∨ ~Ry) ⊃ Wy   2   UI
     7. (Wy ∨ ~Ey) ⊃ ~Sy   3   UI
     8. (Py · My) ⊃ Ly   4   UI

9. Py · My		
10. Ly	8,9	MP
11. Ly ⊃ ~Ry	5	Simp
12. ~Ry	11,10	MP
13. ~Ay ∨ ~Ry	12	Add
14. Wy	6,13	MP
15. Wy ∨ ~Ey	14	Add
16. ~Sy	7,15	MP
17. (Py · My) ⊃ ~Sy	9-16	CP
18. (x)[(Px · Mx) ⊃ ~Sx]	17	UG

62. **1. (x)[Sx ⊃ (Gx ≡ Tx)]**
  2. (x){Tx ⊃ [Ax ∨ (Cx ∨ Nx)]}
  3. (x)[(Tx · Jx) ⊃ ~Cx]
  4. (∃x){[Sx · (Tx · Jx)] · ~Nx}

	/∴	**(∃x){[Sx · (Tx · Jx)] · Ax}**
5. [Sa · (Ta · Ja)] · ~Na	4	EI
6. Ta ⊃ [Aa ∨ (Ca ∨ Na)]	2	UI
7. (Ta · Ja) ⊃ ~Ca	3	UI
8. Sa · (Ta · Ja)	5	Simp
9. ~Na	5	Simp
10. Ta · Ja	8	Simp
11. Ta	10	Simp
12. Aa ∨ (Ca ∨ Na)	6,11	MP
13. ~Ca	7,10	MP
14. ~Ca · ~Na	13,9	Conj
15. ~(Ca ∨ Na)	14	DeM
16. Aa	12,15	DS
17. [Sa · (Ta · Ja)] · Aa	8,16	Conj
18. (∃x){[Sx · (Tx · Jx)] · Ax}	17	EG

Premise one is superfluous.

63. **1. (x)[(Cx · Gx) ⊃ (Rx · Fx)]**
  2. (x)(~Fx ∨ Hx)
  3. (x)(Hx ⊃ ~Sx)
  4. (x)(~Ax ≡ ~Sx) /∴ **(x)[(Cx · Gx) ⊃ ~Ax]**

5.	(Cy · Gy) ⊃ (Ry · Fy)	1	UI
6.	~Fy ∨ Hy	2	UI
7.	Hy ⊃ ~Sy	3	UI
8.	~Ay ≡ ~Sy	4	UI
9.	Cy · Gy		
10.	Ry · Fy	5,9	MP
11.	Fy	10	Simp
12.	Fy ⊃ Hy	6	MI
13.	Hy	12,11	MP
14.	~Sy	7,13	MP
15.	(~Ay ⊃ ~Sy) · (~Sy ⊃ ~Ay)	8	MEA
16.	~Sy ⊃ ~Ay	15	Simp
17.	~Ay	16,14	MP
18.	(Cy · Gy) ⊃ ~Ay	9-17	CP
19.	(x)[(Cx · Gx) ⊃ ~Ax]	18	UG

64.
1.	**(x)[(Bx ∨ Sx) ⊃ (Ax · Vx)]**		
2.	**(∃x)(Fx · ~Vx)**		
3.	**(x)[Fx ⊃ (~Cx ∨ Sx)]**		
4.	**(x)(Sx ⊃ Fx)**	/∴	**(∃x)[Fx · (~Cx · ~Sx)]**
5.	Fa · ~Va	2	EI
6.	(Ba ∨ Sa) ⊃ (Aa · Va)	1	UI
7.	Fa ⊃ (~Ca ∨ Sa)	3	UI
8.	Fa	5	Simp
9.	~Va	5	Simp
10.	~Aa ∨ ~Va	9	Add
11.	~(Aa · Va)	10	DeM
12.	~(Ba ∨ Sa)	6,11	MT
13.	~Ba · ~Sa	12	DeM
14.	~Sa	13	Simp
15.	~Ca ∨ Sa	7,8	MP
16.	~Ca	15,14	DS
17.	~Ca · ~Sa	16,14	Conj
18.	Fa · (~Ca · ~Sa)	8,17	Conj
19.	(∃x)[Fx · (~Cx · ~Sx)]	18	EG

Premise four is superfluous.

65. 1. (x)[(Fx · Ax) ⊃ ~Bx]
     2. (∃x)[(Px · Cx) · Bx]
     3. (x)(Px ⊃ Fx)   /∴   (∃x)[(Fx · Cx) · ~Ax]
     4. (Pa · Ca) · Ba   2   EI
     5. (Fa · Aa) ⊃ ~Ba   1   UI
     6. Pa ⊃ Fa   3   UI
     7. Ba   4   Simp
     8. Pa · Ca   4   Simp
     9. Pa   8   Simp
    10. Fa   6,9   MP
    11. Ca   8   Simp
    12. Fa · Ca   10,11 Conj
    13. ~~Ba   7   DN
    14. ~(Fa · Aa)   5,13   MT
    15. ~Fa ∨ ~Aa   14   DeM
    16. Fa ⊃ ~Aa   15   MI
    17. ~Aa   16,10 MP
    18. (Fa · Ca) · ~Aa   12,17 Conj
    19. (∃x)[(Fx · Cx) · ~Ax]   18   EG

66. 1. (x)[(Ax ∨ Fx) ⊃ (Ex · Cx)]
     2. (x)[(Sx ∨ Ex) ⊃ (Gx · Dx)]
     3. (x)[(Gx ∨ Ix) ⊃ (Yx · Bx)]   /∴   (x)[(Ax ⊃ (Bx ∨ Lx)]
     4. (Ay ∨ Fy) ⊃ (Ey · Cy)   1   UI
     5. (Sy ∨ Ey) ⊃ (Gy · Dy)   2   UI
     6. (Gy ∨ Iy) ⊃ (Yy · By)   3   UI
     7. Ay
     8. Ay ∨ Fy   7   Add
     9. Ey · Cy   4,8   MP
    10. Ey   9   Simp
    11. Sy ∨ Ey   10   Add
    12. Gy · Dy   5,11   MP
    13. Gy   12   Simp
    14. Gy ∨ Iy   13   Add
    15. Yy · By   6,14   MP
    16. By   15   Simp

	17. By ∨ Ly	16	Add
	18. Ay ⊃ (By ∨ Ly)	7-17	CP
	19. (x)[(Ax ⊃ (Bx ∨ Lx)]	18	UG

67. 1. (x)[Cs ⊃ (Nx ∨ Dx)]
2. (x)(Nx ⊃ ~Rx)
3. (x)(Dx ⊃ ~Sx)
4. (x)(Lx ⊃ Rx)   /∴   (x)[(Lx · Sx) ⊃ ~Cx]

	5. Cy ⊃ (Ny ∨ Dy)	1	UI
	6. Ny ⊃ ~Ry	2	UI
	7. Dy ⊃ ~Sy	3	UI
	8. Ly ⊃ Ry	4	UI
	9. Ly · Sy		
	10. Ly	9	Simp
	11. Ry	8,10	MP
	12. Ry ⊃ ~Ny	6	Transp
	13. ~Ny	12,11	MP
	14. Sy	9	Simp
	15. Sy ⊃ ~Dy	7	Transp
	16. ~Dy	15,14	MP
	17. ~Ny · ~Dy	13,16	Conj
	18. ~(Ny ∨ Dy)	17	DeM
	19. ~Cy	5,18	MT
	20. (Ly · Sy) ⊃ ~Cy	9-19	CP
	21. (x)[(Lx · Sx) ⊃ ~Cx]	20	UG

68. 1. (∃x)[(Ex · Fx) · (Bx · Ax)]
2. (x)[(Fx · Px) ⊃ Rx]
3. (x)[~(Px ∨ Sx) ⊃ ~(Bx · Ax)]
4. (x)(Ex ⊃ ~Sx)   /∴   (∃x)(Fx · Rx)

	5. (Ea · Fa) · (Ba · Aa)	1	EI
	6. (Fa · Pa) ⊃ Ra	2	UI
	7. ~(Pa ∨ Sa) ⊃ ~(Ba · Aa)	3	UI
	8. Ea ⊃ ~Sa	4	UI
	9. Ea · Fa	5	Simp
	10. Fa	9	Simp

11.	Fa ⊃ (Pa ⊃ Ra)	6	Export
12.	Pa ⊃ Ra	11,10	MP
13.	(Ba · Aa) ⊃ (Pa ∨ Sa)	7	Transp
14.	Ba · Aa	5	Simp
15.	Pa ∨ Sa	13,14	MP
16.	Ea	9	Simp
17.	~Sa	8,16	MP
18.	Pa	15,17	DS
19.	Ra	12,18	MP
20.	Fa · Ra	10,19	Conj
21.	(∃x)(Fx · Rx)	20	EG

69. **1. (x)(Hx ⊃ Rx)**
    2. (x)(Ax ⊃ Px)
    3. (∃x)(Ax · Mx)
    4. (∃x)(Mx · Ox)
    5. (x)(Hx ⊃ Ox)   /∴   **(x)(Ax ⊃ ~Rx)**

INVALID FOR A UNIVERSE OF ONE OR MORE

Ha	**Ra**	**Aa**	**Pa**	**Ma**	**Oa**
F	T	T	T	T	T

70. **1. (x)[(Fx ∨ Sx) ⊃ Ux]**
    2. (x)[(Ux ∨ Dx) ⊃ Ax]   /∴   **(x)(Fx ⊃ Ax)**

3.	(Fy ∨ Sy) ⊃ Uy	1	UI
4.	(Uy ∨ Dy) ⊃ Ay	2	UI
5.	~Uy ⊃ ~(Fy ∨ Sy)	3	Transp
6.	Uy ∨ ~(Fy ∨ Gy)	5	MI
7.	Uy ∨ (~Fy · ~Gy)	6	DeM
8.	(Uy ∨ ~Fy) · (Uy ∨ ~Gy)	7	Dist
9.	Uy ∨ ~Fy	8	Simp
10.	~Fy ∨ Uy	9	Com
11.	Fy ⊃ Uy	10	MI
12.	~(Uy ∨ Dy) ∨ Ay	4	MI
13.	(~Uy · ~Dy) ∨ Ay	12	DeM

14.	Ay ∨ (~Uy · ~Dy)	13	Com
15.	(Ay ∨ ~Uy) · (Ay ∨ ~Dy)	14	Dist
16.	Ay ∨ ~Uy	15	Simp
17.	~Uy ∨ Ay	16	Com
18.	Uy ⊃ Ay	17	MI
29.	Fy ⊃ Ay	11,18	HS
30.	(x)(Fx ⊃ Ax)	29	UG

71.
1.	**[Ni · (Ei · Bi)] · [Ng · (Eg · Bg)]**		
2.	**(x){[(Nx · Bx) · Ax] ⊃ Tx}**	/∴	**Ag ⊃ (Tg ∨ Sg)**
3.	[(Ng · Bg) · Ag] ⊃ Tg	2	UI
4.	Ng · (Eg · Bg)	1	Simp
5.	Ng	4	Simp
6.	Eg · Bg	4	Simp
7.	Bg	6	Simp
8.	Ng · Bg	5,7	Conj
9.	(Ng · Bg) ⊃ (Ag ⊃ Tg)	3	Export
10.	Ag ⊃ Tg	9,8	MP
11.	~Ag ∨ Tg	10	MI
12.	(~Ag ∨ Tg) ∨ Sg	11	Add
13.	~Ag ∨ (Tg ∨ Sg)	12	Assc
14.	Ag ⊃ (Tg ∨ Sg)	13	MI

72.
1.	**(x)[(Px · Lx) ⊃ ~Rx]**		
2.	**(x)(Nx ⊃ Rx)**		
3.	**(x)[(Px · Hx) ⊃ Nx]**	/∴	**(x)[(Px · Hx) ⊃ ~Lx]**
4.	(Py · Ly) ⊃ ~Ry	1	UI
5.	Ny ⊃ Ry	2	UI
6.	(Py · Hy) ⊃ Ny	3	UI
7.	(Py · Hy) ⊃ Ry	6,5	HS
8.	Ry ⊃ ~(Py · Ly)	4	Transp
9.	(Py · Hy) ⊃ ~(Py · Ly)	7,8	HS
10.	Py · Hy		
11.	~(Py · Ly)	9,10	MP
12.	~Py ∨ ~Ly	11	DeM

13.	Py ⊃ ~Ly	12	MI
14.	Py	10	Simp
15.	~Ly	13,14	MP
16.	(Py · Hy) ⊃ ~Ly	10-15	CP
17.	(x)[(Px · Hx) ⊃ ~Lx]	16	UG

73.
1.	(x)[(Vx · Nx) ⊃ Cx]		
2.	(x)(Fx ⊃ Px)		
3.	(x)[(Cx · Px) ⊃ Sx] /∴ (x){[Vx · (Fx · Nx)] ⊃ (Cx · Sx)}		
4.	(Vy · Ny) ⊃ Cy	1	UI
5.	Fy ⊃ Py	2	UI
6.	(Cy · Py) ⊃ Sy	3	UI
7.	Vy · (Fy · Ny)		
8.	Vy · (Ny · Fy)	7	Com
9.	(Vy · Ny) · Fy	8	Assc
10.	Vy · Ny	9	Simp
11.	Cy	4,10	MP
12.	Fy	9	Simp
13.	Py	5,12	MP
14.	Cy · Py	11,13	Conj
15.	Sy	6,14	MP
16.	Cy · Sy	11,15	Conj
17.	[Vy · (Fy · Ny)] ⊃ (Cy · Sy)	7-16	CP
18.	(x)[[Vx · (Fx · Nx)] ⊃ (Cx · Sx)}	17	UG

74.
1.	(x){Tx ⊃ [Bx ∨ (Sx ∨ Px)]}		
2.	(x)(Bx ⊃ Cx)		
3.	(x)(Sx ⊃ Fx)		
4.	(x)(Px ⊃ Dx)		
5.	(∃x)(Tx)	/∴	(∃x)[Cx ∨ (Fx ∨ Dx)]
6.	Ta	5	EI
7.	Ta ⊃ [Ba ∨ (Sa ∨ Pa)]	1	UI
8.	Ba ⊃ Ca	2	UI
9.	Sa ⊃ Fa	3	UI
10.	Pa ⊃ Da	4	UI
11.	Ba ∨ (Sa ∨ Pa)	7,6	MP

12.	~Ba ⊃ (Sa ∨ Pa)	11	MI
13.	(Sa ⊃ Fa) ∨ Da	9	Add
14.	(~Sa ∨ Fa) ∨ Da	13	MI
15.	~Sa ∨ (Fa ∨ Da)	14	Assc
16.	(Pa ⊃ Da) ∨ Fa	10	Add
17.	(~Pa ∨ Da) ∨ Fa	16	MI
18.	~Pa ∨ (Da ∨ Fa)	17	Assc
19.	~Pa ∨ (Fa ∨ Da)	18	Com
20.	[~Sa ∨ (Fa ∨ Da)] · [~Pa ∨ (Fa ∨ Da)]	15,19	Conj
21.	[(Fa ∨ Da) ∨ ~Sa] · [(Fa ∨ Da) ∨ ~Pa]	20	Com
22.	(Fa ∨ Da) ∨ (~Sa · ~Pa)	21	Dist
23.	(~Sa · ~Pa) ∨ (Fa ∨ Da)	22	Com
24.	~(Sa ∨ Pa) ∨ (Fa ∨ Da)	23	DeM
25.	(Sa ∨ Pa) ⊃ (Fa ∨ Da)	24	MI
26.	~Ba ⊃ (Fa ∨ Da)	12,25	HS
27.	~Ca ⊃ ~Ba	8	Transp
28.	~Ca ⊃ (Fa ∨ Da)	27,26	HS
29.	Ca ∨ (Fa ∨ Da)	28	MI
30.	(∃x)[Cx ∨ (Fx ∨ Dx)]	29	EG

If "constructive trilemma" were a standard rule, this would not be quite so tricky. Using Conditional Proof would also shorten things by thirteen lines. How would you set one up?

75.	1.	(x)(Tx ⊃ Px)		
	2.	(x)(Tx ∨ Sx)		
	3.	(∃x)(Gx · ~Tx)		
	4.	(x)(Sx ⊃ Lx)		
	5.	~(∃x)(Px · Lx)	/∴	(∃x)[Gx · (~Px · Lx)]
	6.	(x)~(Px · Lx)	5	QN
	7.	Ga · ~Ta	3	EI
	8.	Tx ⊃ Pa	1	UI
	9.	Ta ∨ Sa	2	UI
	10.	Sa ⊃ La	4	UI
	11.	~(Pa · La)	6	UI
	12.	Ga	7	Simp

13. ~Ta	7	Simp
14. Sa	9,13	DS
15. La	10,14	MP
16. ~Pa ∨ ~La	11	DeM
17. Pa ⊃ ~La	16	MI
18. La ⊃ ~Pa	17	Transp
19. ~Pa	18,15	MP
20. ~Pa · La	19,15	Conj
21. Ga · (~Pa · La)	12,20	Conj
22. (∃x)[Gx · (~Px · Lx)]	21	EG

76. **RESTRICTED DOMAIN: x = GM car.**

1. **(x)(Ax ≡ Lx)**		
2. **(∃x)[Ax · (Bx · ~Cx)]**		
3. **(x)(Bx ⊃ Rx)**		
4. **(x)(Cx ∨ Ox)**		
5. **(x)[(Ox · Rx) ⊃ Tx]**	/∴	**(∃x)(Lx · Tx)**
6. Aa · (Ba · ~Ca)	2	EI
7. Aa ≡ La	1	UI
8. Ba ⊃ Ra	3	UI
9. Ca ∨ Oa	4	UI
10. (Oa · Ra) ⊃ Ta	5	UI
11. (Aa ⊃ La) · (La ⊃ Aa)	7	MEA
12. Aa ⊃ La	11	Simp
13. Aa	6	Simp
14. La	12,13	MP
15. Ba · ~Ca	6	Simp
16. Ba	15	Simp
17. Ra	8,16	MP
18. ~Ca	15	Simp
19. Oa	9,18	DS
20. Oa · Ra	19,17	Conj
21. Ta	10,20	MP
22. La · Ta	14,21	Conj
23. (∃x)(Lx · Tx)	22	EG

77.   1. (x){Ux ⊃ [(Gx ∨ Ix) · ~(Gx · Ix)]}
     2. (x){Gx ⊃ [(Fx ∨ Sx) · ~(Fx · Sx)]}
     3. (x){Gx ⊃ [(Ox · Cx) ⊃ Sx]}
                /∴   (x){(Ux · ~Ix) ⊃ [(Ox · Cx) ⊃ ~Fx]}

4. Uy ⊃ [(Gy ∨ Iy) · ~(Gy · Iy)]	1	UI
5. Gy ⊃ [(Fy ∨ Sy) · ~(Fy · Sy)]	2	UI
6. Gy ⊃ [(Oy · Cy) ⊃ Sy]	3	UI
7. Uy · ~Iy		
8. Oy · Cy		
9. Uy	7	Simp
10. (Gy ∨ Iy) · ~(Gy · Iy)	4,9	MP
11. Gy ∨ Iy	10	Simp
12. ~Iy	7	Simp
13. Gy	11,12	DS
14. (Oy · Cy) ⊃ Sy	6,13	MP
15. Sy	14,8	MP
16. (Fy ∨ Sy) · ~(Fy · Sy)	5,13	MP
17. ~(Fy · Sy)	16	Simp
18. ~Fy ∨ ~Sy	17	DeM
19. ~Sy ∨ ~Fy	18	Com
20. Sy ⊃ ~Fy	19	MI
21. ~Fy	20,15	MP
22. (Oy · Cy) ⊃ ~Fy	8-21	CP
23. (Uy · ~Iy) ⊃ [(Oy · Cy) ⊃ ~Fy]	7-22	CP
24. (x){(Ux · ~Ix) ⊃ [(Ox · Cx) ⊃ ~Fx]}	23	UG

78.   1. (x){Ax ⊃ [~Px ∨ (Fx · Lx)]}
     2. (x)[~Cx ∨ (Sx · Rx)]
     3. (x)(Fx ⊃ ~Sx)
     4. (x)(Rx ⊃ ~Lx)   /∴ (x){[Ax · (Px · Cx)] ⊃ Ex}

5. Ay ⊃ [~Py ∨ (Fy · Ly)]	1	UI
6. ~Cy ∨ (Sy · Ry)	2	UI
7. Fy ⊃ ~Sy	3	UI
8. Ry ⊃ ~Ly	4	UI
9. (Ay · Py) ⊃ (Fy · Ly)	5	Export
10. ~(Ay · Py) ∨ (Fy · Ly)	9	MI

11.	[~(Ay · Py) ∨ Fy] · [~(Ay · Py) ∨ Ly]	10	Dist
12.	~(Ay · Py) ∨ Fy	11	Simp
13.	(Ay · Py) ⊃ Fy	12	MI
14.	(Ay · Py) ⊃ ~Sy	13,7	HS
15.	(~Cy ∨ Sy) · (~Cy ∨ Ry)	6	Dist
16.	~Cy ∨ Sy	15	Simp
17.	Cy ⊃ Sy	16	MI
18.	~Sy ⊃ ~Cy	17	Transp
19.	(Ay · Py) ⊃ ~Cy	14,18	HS
20.	~(Ay · Py) ∨ ~Cy	19	MI
21.	(~Ay ∨ ~Py) ∨ ~Cy	20	DeM
22.	~Ay ∨ (~Py ∨ ~Cy)	21	Assc
23.	~Ay ∨ ~(Py · Cy)	22	DeM
24.	~[Ay · (Py · Cy)]	23	DeM
25.	~[Ay · (Py · Cy)] ∨ Ey	24	Add
26.	[Ay · (Py · Cy)] ⊃ Ey	25	MI
27.	(x){[Ax · (Px · Cx)] ⊃ Ex}	26	UG

Since the antecedent of the conclusion contradicts the stand-ing premises, the use of conditional proof is interesting, though no shorter. From line nine, it goes as follows:

9.	Ay · (Py · Cy)		
10.	Ay	9	Simp
11.	~Py ∨ (Fy · Ly)	5,10	MP
12.	Py ⊃ (Fy · Ly)	11	MI
13.	Py · Cy	9	Simp
14.	Py	13	Simp
15.	Fy · Ly	12,14	MP
16.	Fy	15	Simp
17.	~Sy	7,16	MP
18.	Ly ⊃ ~Ry	8	Transp
19.	Ly	15	Simp
20.	~Ry	18,19	MP
21.	~Sy · ~Ry	17,20	Conj
22.	~(Sy ∨ Ry)	21	DeM
*23.	~Cy	6,22	DS

*24. Cy	13	Simp
25. Cy ∨ Ey	24	Add
26. Ey	25,23	DS
27. [Ay · (Py · Cy)] ⊃ Ey	9-26	CP
28. (x){[Ax · (Px · Cx)] ⊃ Ex}	27	UG

79. **RESTRICTED DOMAIN:** x = computers.

1. (x)[(Fx ∨ Lx) ⊃ Rx]		
2. (x)[~Rx ∨ (Px ∨ Kx)]		
3. (x)(Px ⊃ Ax)		
4. (x)(Lx ⊃ ~Ax)		
5. (x)(Kx ⊃ Vx)		
6. (x)[Vx ⊃ (~Sx ∨ Ex)]		
7. (x)[(Fx ∨ Lx) ⊃ Sx]	/∴	**(x)(Lx ⊃ Ex)**
8. (Fy ∨ Ly) ⊃ Ry	1	UI
9. ~Ry ∨ (Py ∨ Ky)	2	UI
10. Py ⊃ Ay	3	UI
11. Ly ⊃ ~Ay	4	UI
12. Ky ⊃ Vy	5	UI
13. Vy ⊃ (~Sy ∨ Ey)	6	UI
14. (Fy ∨ Ly) ⊃ Sy	7	UI
15. Ly		
16. Fy ∨ Ly	15	Add
17. Sy	14,16	MP
18. Ry	8,16	MP
19. Ry ⊃ (Py ∨ Ky)	9	MI
20. Py ∨ Ky	19,18	MP
21. ~Ay	11,15	MP
22. ~Py	10,21	MT
23. Ky	20,22	DS
24. Vy	12,23	MP
25. ~Sy ∨ Ey	13,24	MP
26. Sy ⊃ Ey	25	MI
27. Ey	26,17	MP
28. Ly ⊃ Ey	15-27	CP
29. (x)(Lx ⊃ Ex)	28	UG

80.
1.	(x)(Bx ⊃ Sx)		/∴	(x)[Wx ⊃ (Ex ∨ ~Ex)]
2.	By ⊃ Sy		1	UI
3.	~Ey ∨ (By ⊃ Sy)		2	Add
4.	Ey ⊃ (By ⊃ Sy)		3	MI
5.	Ey ⊃ [Ey · (By ⊃ Sy)]		4	Abs
6.	~Ey ∨ [Ey · (By ⊃ Sy)]		5	MI
7.	(~Ey ∨ Ey) · [~Ey ∨ (By ⊃ Sy)]		6	Dist
8.	~Ey ∨ Ey		7	Simp
9.	Ey ∨ ~Ey		8	Com
10.	~Wy ∨ (Ey ∨ ~Ey)		9	Add
11.	Wy ⊃ (Ey ∨ ~Ey)		10	MI
12.	(x)[Wx ⊃ (Ex ∨ ~Ex)]		11	UG

Quantifiers are not really necessary for this problem. Indeed, you have done it before without them. The level to which analysis should be carried in symbolizing sentences depends on the context and the comnplexity of the argument in which they occur. There are arguments in which 'Everybody loves somebody sometime' could be symbolized effectively as L. In more complex settings, the same sentence can take at least three quantifiers.

81.
1.	(x)[(Ex ∨ Hx) ⊃ Sx]		
2.	Eb · (Ib · Ab)		
3.	(x)(Gx ⊃ ~Mx)		
4.	(x)(Cx ⊃ Gx)		
5.	(x)[(Sx · ~Mx) ⊃ Lx]		
6.	(x)[(Ix · Tx) ⊃ Cx]	/∴	Tb ⊃ Lb
7.	(Eb ∨ Hb) ⊃ Sb	1	UI
8.	Gb ⊃ ~Mb	3	UI
9.	Cb ⊃ Gb	4	UI
10.	(Sb · ~Mb) ⊃ Lb	5	UI
11.	(Ib · Tb) ⊃ Cb	6	UI
12.	Eb	2	Simp
13.	Eb ∨ Hb	12	Add
14.	Sb	7,13	MP
15.	Sb ⊃ (~Mb ⊃ Lb)	10	Export

16. ~Mb ⊃ Lb	15,14	MP
17. Gb ⊃ Lb	8,16	HS
18. Cb ⊃ Lb	9,17	HS
19. Ib · Ab	2	Simp
20. Ib	19	Simp
21. Ib ⊃ (Tb ⊃ Cb)	11	Export
22. Tb ⊃ Cb	21,20	MP
23. Tb ⊃ Lb	22,18	HS

82.
1. **(x)[(Sx ∨ Mx) ⊃ (Dx · Ox)]**
2. **(x)(Dx ⊃ Vx)**
3. **(x)[~Vx ∨ (Gx · Px)]**
4. **(x)(Px ≡ Sx)**   /∴   **(x)[(Sx ∨ Dx) ⊃ (Sx · Dx)]**

5. (Sy ∨ My) ⊃ (Dy · Oy)	1	UI
6. Dy ⊃ Vy	2	UI
7. ~Vy ∨ (Gy · Py)	3	UI
8. Py ≡ Sy	4	UI
9. Sy		
10. Sy ∨ My	9	Add
11. Dy · Oy	5,10	MP
12. Dy	11	Simp
13. Sy ⊃ Dy	9-12	CP
14. Dy		
15. Vy	6,14	MP
16. Vy ⊃ (Gy · Py)	7	MI
17. Gy · Py	16,15	MP
18. Py	17	Simp
19. (Py ⊃ Sy) · (Sy ⊃ Py)	8	MEA
20. Py ⊃ Sy	19	Simp
21. Sy	20,18	MP
22. Dy ⊃ Sy	14-21	CP
23. (Sy ⊃ Dy) · (Dy ⊃ Sy)	13,22	Conj
24. Sy ≡ Dy	23	MEA
25. (Sy · Dy) ∨ (~Sy · ~Dy)	24	MEB
26. (Sy · Dy) ∨ ~(Sy ∨ Dy)	25	DeM
27. ~(Sy ∨ Dy) ∨ (Sy · Dy)	26	Com

28.	(Sy ∨ Dy) ⊃ (Sy · Dy)	27	MI
29.	(x)[(Sx ∨ Dx) ⊃ (Sx · Dx)]	28	UG

83.
1.	**(x)(Lx ⊃ Fx)**		
2.	**(x)(Ox ⊃ Gx)**	/∴	**(x)(Lx ∨ Ox) ⊃ (x)(Fx ∨ Gx)**
3.	Ly ⊃ Fy	1	UI
4.	Oy ⊃ Gy	2	UI
5.	(x)(Lx ∨ Ox)		
6.	Ly ∨ Oy	5	UI
7.	(Ly ⊃ Fy) · (Oy ⊃ Gy)	3,4	Conj
8.	Fy ∨ Gy	7,6	CD
9.	(x)(Fx ∨ Gx)	8	UG
10.	(x)(Lx ∨ Ox) ⊃ (x)(Fx ∨ Gx)	5-9	CP

84.
1.	**(x)(Zx ⊃ Kx)**		
2.	**(x)[Kx ⊃ (Sx · Cx)]**		
3.	**(x)(Cx ≡ Hx)**		
*4.	**Kt**		
5.	**(x)(Kx ⊃ ~Hx)**	/∴	**Mt**
6.	Zt ⊃ Kt	1	UI
7.	Kt ⊃ (St · Ct)	2	UI
8.	Ct ≡ Ht	3	UI
9.	Kt ⊃ ~Ht	5	UI
10.	(Ct ⊃ Ht) · (Ht ⊃ Ct)	8	MEA
11.	Ct ⊃ Ht	10	Simp
12.	~Ht ⊃ ~Ct	11	Transp
13.	Kt ⊃ ~Ct	9,12	HS
14.	~Kt ∨ (St · Ct)	7	MI
15.	(~Kt ∨ St) · (~Kt ∨ Ct)	14	Dist
16.	~Kt ∨ Ct	15	Simp
17.	Kt ⊃ Ct	16	MI
18.	~Ct ⊃ ~Kt	17	Transp
19.	Kt ⊃ ~Kt	13,18	HS
20.	~Kt ∨ ~Kt	19	MI
*21.	~Kt	20	Taut

22. Kt ∨ Mt	4	Add
23. Mt	22,21	DS

*VALID BUT UNSOUND; INCONSISTENT PREMISES.

85. 1. **(x)[Ex ≡ ~(Mx · Ax)]**
    2. **~(x)(Ax ⊃ ~Ex)**
    3. **(x)[Ax ⊃ (Mx ∨ Fx)]**   /∴   **(∃x)[(Ax · Fx) · Ex]**

4. (∃x)~(Ax ⊃ ~Ex)	2	QN
5. ~(Aa ⊃ ~Ea)	4	EI
6. Ea ≡ ~(Ma · Aa)	1	UI
7. Aa ⊃ (Ma ∨ Fa)	3	UI
8. ~(~Aa ∨ ~Ea)	5	MI
9. Aa · Ea	8	DeM
10. Aa	9	Simp
11. Ma ∨ Fa	7,10	MP
12. [Ea ⊃ ~(Ma · Aa)] · [~(Ma · Aa) ⊃ Ea]	6	MEA
13. Ea ⊃ ~(Ma · Aa)	12	Simp
14. Ea	9	Simp
15. ~(Ma · Aa)	13,14	MP
16. ~Ma ∨ ~Aa	15	DeM
17. ~~Aa	10	DN
18. ~Ma	16,17	DS
19. Fa	11,18	DS
20. Aa · Fa	10,19	Conj
21. (Aa · Fa) · Ea	20,14	Conj
22. (∃x)[(Ax · Fx) · Ex]	21	EG

86. 1. **(x){[(Ax · Cx) · Gx] ⊃ Fx}**
    2. **(x){[Cx · ~(Bx ∨ Wx)] ⊃ ~(Ax · ~Gx)}**
    3. **(x)(Cx ⊃ Ax)**
    4. **(x)(Ax ⊃ ~Wx)**
    5. **(∃x)(Cx · ~Fx)**   /∴   **(∃x)(Cx · Bx)**

6. Ca · ~Fa	5	EI
7. [(Aa · Ca) · Ga] ⊃ Fa	1	UI
8. [Ca · ~(Ba ∨ Wa)] ⊃ ~(Aa · ~Ga)	2	UI

9. Ca ⊃ Aa	3	UI
10. Aa ⊃ ~Wa	4	UI
11. Ca	6	Simp
12. ~Fa	6	Simp
13. ~[(Aa · Ca) · Ga]	7,12	MT
14. ~[Aa · (Ca · Ga)]	13	Assc
15. ~Aa ∨ ~(Ca · Ga)	14	DeM
16. Aa ⊃ ~(Ca · Ga)	15	MI
17. Aa	9,11	MP
18. ~(Ca · Ga)	16,17	MP
19. ~Ca ∨ ~Ga	18	DeM
20. Ca ⊃ ~Ga	19	MI
21. ~Ga	20,11	MP
22. Aa · ~Ga	17,21	Conj
23. ~~(Aa · ~Ga)	22	DN
24. ~[Ca · ~(Ba ∨ Wa)]	8,23	MT
25. ~Ca ∨ (Ba ∨ Wa)	24	DeM
26. Ca ⊃ (Ba ∨ Wa)	25	MI
27. Ba ∨ Wa	26,11	MP
28. ~Wa	10,17	MP
29. Ba	27,28	DS
30. Ca · Ba	11,29	Conj
31. (∃x)(Cx · Bx)	30	EG

87.
1. (x)([Hx ⊃ (Px · Sx)]		
2. (x)(Px ⊃ ~Mx)		
3. (∃x)(Ux · Mx)		
4. (x)(Cx ⊃ Ix)		
5. (x)(~Ux ∨ Cx)		
6. (x)[(~Hx · Ix) ⊃ Ax]	/∴	(∃x)(Ax · Ux)
7. Ua · Ma	3	EI
8. Ha ⊃ (Pa · Sa)	1	UI
9. Pa ⊃ ~Ma	2	UI
10. Ca ⊃ Ia	4	UI
11. ~Ua ∨ Ca	5	UI

12.	(~Ha · Ia) ⊃ Aa	6	UI
13.	Ua ⊃ Ca	11	MI
14.	Ua	7	Simp
15.	Ca	13,14	MP
16.	Ia	10,15	MP
17.	Ma	7	Simp
18.	Ma ⊃ ~Pa	9	Transp
19.	~Pa	18,17	MP
20.	~Pa ∨ ~Sa	19	Add
21.	~(Pa · Sa)	20	DeM
22.	~Ha	8,21	MT
23.	~Ha · Ia	22,16	Conj
24.	Aa	12,23	MP
25.	Aa · Ua	24,14	Conj
26.	(∃x)(Ax · Ux)	25	EG

88. **RESTRICTED DOMAIN: x = pure-bred dog.**

1.	**(x)(Qx ≡ Ax)**		
2.	**(∃x)[Qx · (Lx · ~Tx)]**		
3.	**(x)(Lx ⊃ Sx)**		
4.	**(x)(Tx ∨ Rx)**		
5.	**(x)[(Rx · Sx) ⊃ Cx]**	/∴	**(∃x)(Ax · Cx)**
6.	Qa · (La · ~Ta)	2	EI
7.	Qa ≡ Aa	1	UI
8.	La ⊃ Sa	3	UI
9.	Ta ∨ Ra	4	UI
10.	(Ra · Sa) ⊃ Ca	5	UI
11.	La · ~Ta	6	Simp
12.	La	11	Simp
13.	Sa	8,12	MP
14.	~Ta	11	Simp
15.	Ra	9,14	DS
16.	Ra · Sa	15,13	Conj
17.	Ca	10,16	MP
18.	Qa	6	Simp

19. (Qa ⊃ Aa) · (Aa ⊃ Qa)	7	MEA
20. Qa ⊃ Aa	19	Simp
21. Aa	20,18	MP
22. Aa · Ca	21,17	Conj
23. (∃x)(Ax · Cx)	21	EG

89.
1. (∃x)(Gx · Vx)		
2. (x)(Gx ⊃ ~Tx)		
3. (x)[(Gx ∨ Fx) ⊃ (Sx · Bx)]		
4. (x){[Bx · (Vx · ~Tx)] ⊃ (Cx ∨ Mx)}		
5. (x)[(Ox ∨ Gx) ⊃ ~Cx]	/∴	**(∃x)(Gx · Mx)**
6. Ga · Va	1	EI
7. Ga ⊃ ~Ta	2	UI
8. (Ga ∨ Fa) ⊃ (Sa · Ba)	3	UI
9. [Ba · (Va · ~Ta)] ⊃ (Ca ∨ Ma)	4	UI
10. (Oa ∨ Ga) ⊃ ~Ca	5	UI
11. Ga	6	Simp
12. Va	6	Simp
13. ~Ta	7,11	MP
14. Ga ∨ Fa	11	Add
15. Sa · Ba	8,14	MP
16. Ba	15	Simp
17. Ba · Va	16,12	Conj
18. (Ba · Va) · ~Ta	17,13	Conj
19. Ca ∨ Ma	9,18	MP
20. Oa ∨ Ga	11	Add
21. ~Ca	10,20	MP
22. Ma	19,21	DS
23. Ga · Ma	11,22	Conj
24. (∃x)(Gx · Mx)	23	EG

90.
1. (x)(STx ⊃ Tx)
2. (x)(SNx ⊃ Gx)
3. (x){SQx ⊃ [STx · (SNx · SKx)]}
4. (x){[(Gx · Tx) · SKx] ⊃ ~Dx}

5.	(x)(SQx ⊃ ~Kx)		
6.	(x)[(~Dx · ~Kx) ⊃ Mx]	/∴	(x)(SQx ⊃ Mx)
7.	STy ⊃ Ty	1	UI
8.	SNy ⊃ Gy	2	UI
9.	SQy ⊃ [STy · (SNy · SKy)]	3	UI
10.	[(Gy · Ty) · SKy] ⊃ ~Dy	4	UI
11.	SQy ⊃ ~Ky	5	UI
12.	(~Dy · ~Ky) ⊃ My	6	UI

13.	SQy		
14.	STy · (SNy · SKy)	9,13	MP
15.	STy	14	Simp
16.	Ty	7,15	MP
17.	SNy · SKy	14	Simp
18.	SNy	17	Simp
19.	Gy	8,18	MP
20.	Gy · Ty	19,16	Conj
21.	SKy	17	Simp
22.	(Gy · Ty) · SKy	20,21	Conj
23.	~Dy	10,22	MP
24.	~Ky	11,13	MP
25.	~Dy · ~Ky	23,24	Conj
26.	My	12,25	MP
27.	SQy ⊃ My	13-26	CP
28.	(x)(SQx ⊃ Mx)	27	UG

NOTE: Kx = "x may be legally killed"

91.	1.	(x){Fx ⊃ [Dx ≡ (Ax ∨ Px)]}		
	2.	(x)(Bx ⊃ ~Dx)	/∴	(x)[Fx ⊃ ~(Px · Bx)]
	3.	Fy ⊃ [Dy ≡ (Ay ∨ Py)]	1	UI
	4.	By ⊃ ~Dy	2	UI
	5.	Fy		
	6.	Dy ≡ (Ay ∨ Py)	3,5	MP
	7.	[Dy ⊃ (Ay ∨ Py)] · [(Ay ∨ Py) ⊃ Dy]	6	MEA
	8.	(Ay ∨ Py) ⊃ Dy	7	Simp
	9.	~(Ay ∨ Py) ∨ Dy	8	MI
	10.	Dy ∨ ~(Ay ∨ Py)	9	com

11. Dy ∨ (~Ay · ~Py)	10	DeM
12. (Dy ∨ ~Ay) · (Dy ∨ ~Py)	11	Dist
13. Dy ∨ ~Py	12	Simp
14. ~Py ∨ Dy	13	Com
15. Py ⊃ Dy	14	MI
16. Dy ⊃ ~By	4	Transp
17. Py ⊃ ~By	15,16	HS
18. ~Py ∨ ~By	17	MI
19. ~(Py · Bx)	18	DeM
20. Fy ⊃ ~(Py · By)	5-19	CP
21. (x)[Fx ⊃ ~(Px · Bx)]	20	UG

A further conditional proof can reduce this by another three lines, as follows:

9. Py		
10. Ay ∨ Py	9	Add
11. Dy	8,10	MP
12. Dy ⊃ ~By	4	Transp
13. ~By	12,11	MP
14. Py ⊃ ~By	9-13	CP
15. ~Py ∨ ~By	14	MI
16. ~(Py · By)	15	DeM
17. Fy ⊃ ~(Py · By)	5-17	CP
18. (x)[Fx ⊃ ~(Px · Bx)]	17	UG

92.
1. (x){[Ax ∨ (Ox ∨ Gx)] ⊃ [Dx · (Nx · Hx)]}		
2. (x)[(Nx ∨ Fx) ⊃ (Vx · Mx)]		
3. (x){Ox ⊃ [Mx ⊃ (Ex ⊃ Lx)]}		
4. (x)(Ox ⊃ Px) /∴ **(x){Ox ⊃ [Px ≡ (Ex ⊃ Lx)]}**		
5. [Ay ∨ (Oy ∨ Gy)] ⊃ [Dy · (Ny · Hy)]	1	UI
6. (Ny ∨ Fy) ⊃ (Vy · My)	2	UI
7. Oy ⊃ [My ⊃ (Ey ⊃ Ly)]	3	UI
8. Oy ⊃ Py	4	UI
9. Oy		
10. Py	8,9	MP
11. My ⊃ (Ey ⊃ Ly)	7,9	MP

12. Oy ∨ Gy	9	Add
13. Ay ∨ (Oy ∨ Gy)	12	Add
14. Dy · (Ny · Hy)	5,13	MP
15. Ny · Hy	14	Simp
16. Ny	15	Simp
17. Ny ∨ Fy	16	Add
18. Vy · My	6,17	MP
19. My	18	Simp
20. Ey ⊃ Ly	11,19	MP
21. Py · (Ey ⊃ Ly)	10,20	Conj
22. [Py · (Ey ⊃ Ly)] ∨ [~Py · ~(Ey ⊃ Ly)]	21	Add
23. Py ≡ (Ey ⊃ Ly)	22	MEB
24. Oy ⊃ [Py ≡ (Ey ⊃ Ly)]	9-23	CP
25. (x){Ox ⊃ [Px ≡ (Ex ⊃ Lx)]}	24	UG

93. **1. (x)(Lx ⊃ Wx)**
　　 2. (x)[(Ex ∨ Bx) ⊃ Px]
　　 3. (x)(Rx ⊃ Hx)
　　　　　　　/∴ (x){~[Px ∨ (Hx ∨ Wx)] ⊃ ~[Lx ∨ (Rx ∨ Ex)]}

4. Ly ⊃ Wy	1	UI
5. (Ey ∨ By) ⊃ Py	2	UI
6. Ry ⊃ Hy	3	UI
7. Ey		
8. Ey ∨ By	7	Add
9. Py	5,8	MP
10. Ey ⊃ Py	7-9	CP
11. (Ry ⊃ Hy) · (Ey ⊃ Py)	6,10	Conj
12. Ry ∨ Ey		
13. Hy ∨ Py	11,12	CD
14. (Ry ∨ Ey) ⊃ (Hy ∨ Py)	12-13	CP
15. (Ly ⊃ Wy) · [(Ry ∨ Ey) ⊃ (Hy ∨ Py)]	4,14	Conj
16. Ly ∨ (Ry ∨ Ey)		
17. Wy ∨ (Hy ∨ Py)	15,16	CD
18. (Wy ∨ Hy) ∨ Py	17	Assc
19. Py ∨ (Wy ∨ Hy)	18	Com
20. Py ∨ (Hy ∨ Wy)	29	Com
21. [Ly ∨ (Ry ∨ Ey)] ⊃ [Py ∨ (Hy ∨ Wy)]	16-20	CP

22. ~[Py ∨ (Hy ∨ Wy)] ⊃ ~[Ly ∨ (Ry ∨ Ey)]	21	Transp
23. (x){~[Px ∨ (Hx ∨ Wx)] ⊃ ~[Lx ∨ (Rx ∨ Ex)]}	22	UG

94. **1 ~(x)(Px ⊃ Wx)**
  2. (x)[Px ⊃ (Bx ⊃ Ix)]
  3. (x)[Lx ⊃ (Bx · Px)]
  4. (x)(Ix ⊃ Wx)   /∴ **(∃x)(Px · ~Lx)**
  5. (∃x)~(Px ⊃ Wx)   1   QN
  6. ~(Pa ⊃ Wa)   5   EI
  7. Pa ⊃ (Ba ⊃ Ia)   2   UI
  8. La ⊃ (Ba · Pa)   3   UI
  9. Ia ⊃ Wa   4   UI
  10. ~(~Pa ∨ Wa)   6   MI
  11. Pa · ~Wa   10   DeM
  12. Pa   11   Simp
  13. Ba ⊃ Ia   7,12   MP
  14. ~Wa   11   Simp
  15. ~Ia   9,14   MT
  16. ~Ba   13,15   MT
  17. ~Ba ∨ ~Pa   16   Add
  18. ~(Ba · Pa)   17   DeM
  19. ~La   8,18   MT
  20. Pa · ~La   12,19   Conj
  21. (∃x)(Px · ~Lx)   20   EG

95. **1. (x)[(Fx ∨ Sx) ⊃ (Nx · Ix)]**
  2. (x)[Ax ⊃ ~(Nx ∨ Ix)]
  3. (∃x)[(Ux · Wx) · Ax]
  4. (x){Ux ⊃ [(Fx ∨ Sx) ∨ (Jx ∨ SRx)]}
  5. (x)(~Nx ⊃ Cx)   /∴ **(∃x){Wx · [(Jx ∨ SRx) · Cx]}**
  6. (Ua · Wa) · Aa   3   EI
  7. (Fa ∨ Sa) ⊃ (Na · Ia)   1   UI
  8. Aa ⊃ ~(Na ∨ Ia)   2   UI
  9. Ua ⊃ [(Fa ∨ Sa) ∨ (Ja ∨ SRa)]   4   UI
  10. ~Na ⊃ Ca   5   UI

11.	Ua · Wa	6	Simp
12.	Wa	11	Simp
13.	Ua	11	Simp
14.	(Fa ∨ Sa) ∨ (Ja ∨ SRa)	9,13	MP
15.	Aa	6	Simp
16.	~(Na ∨ Ia)	8,15	MP
17.	~Na · ~Ia	16	DeM
18.	~Na	17	Simp
19.	~Na ∨ ~Ia	18	Add
20.	~(Na · Ia)	19	DeM
21.	~(Fa ∨ Sa)	7,20	MT
22.	Ja ∨ SRa	14,21	DS
23.	Wa · (Ja ∨ SRa)	12,22	Conj
24.	Ca	10,18	MP
25.	[Wa · (Ja ∨ SRa)] · Ca	23,24	Conj
26.	Wa · [(Ja ∨ SRa) · Ca]	25	Assc
27.	(∃x){Wx · [(Jx ∨ SRx) · Cx]}	26	EG

96.
1.	**(x)[Ax ⊃ (Ex ∨ Cx)]**		
2.	**(x)(Ix ⊃ ~Ex)**		
3.	**(x)[~Ix ⊃ (Cx · Mx)]**		
4.	**(x)[(Cx ∨ Hx) ⊃ (Gx ∨ ~Sx)]**		
5.	**(x)[Gx ⊃ (Ax · Tx)]** /∴	**(x)[Sx ⊃ (Ax ≡ Cx)]**	
6.	Ay ⊃ (Ey ∨ Cy)	1	UI
7.	Iy ⊃ ~Ey	2	UI
8.	~Iy ⊃ (Cy · My)	3	UI
9.	(Cy ∨ Hy) ⊃ (Gy ∨ ~Sy)	4	UI
10.	Gy ⊃ (Ay · Ty)	5	UI
11.	Sy		
12.	Ay		
13.	Ey ∨ Cy	6,12	MP
14.	Cy ∨ Ey	13	Com
15.	~Cy ⊃ Ey	14	MI
16.	Ey ⊃ ~Iy	7	Transp
17.	~Cy ⊃ ~Iy	15,16	HS
18.	~Cy ⊃ (Cy · My)	17,8	HS

19. Cy ∨ (Cy · My)	18	MI
20. (Cy ∨ Cy) · (Cy ∨ My)	19	Dist
21. Cy ∨ Cy	20	Simp
22. Cy	21	Taut
23. Ay ⊃ Cy	12-22	CP
24. Cy		
25. Cy ∨ Hy	24	Add
26. Gy ∨ ~Sy	9,25	MP
27. ~~Sy	11	DN
28. Gy	26,27	DS
29. Ay · Ty	10,28	MP
30. Ay	29	Simp
31. Cy ⊃ Ay	24-30	CP
32. (Ay ⊃ Cy) · (Cy ⊃ Ay)	23,31	Conj
33. Ay ≡ Cy	32	MEA
34. Sy ⊃ (Ay ≡ Cy)	11-33	CP
35. (x)[Sx ⊃ (Ax ≡ Cx)]	34	UG

97.

1. (x)(Tx ⊃ Dx)		
2. (∃x)(Tx · Yx)	/∴	~(x)(Dx ⊃ ~Yx)
3. Ta · Ya	2	EI
4. Ta	3	Simp
5. Ta ⊃ Da	1	UI
6. Da	5,4	MP
7. Ya	3	Simp
8. Da · Ya	6,7	Conj
9. ~(~Da ∨ ~Ya)	8	DeM
10. ~(Da ⊃ ~Ya)	9	MI
11. (∃x)~(Da ⊃ ~Ya)	10	EG
12. ~(x)(Da ⊃ ~Ya)	11	QN

98.

1. (x)(Fx ≡ Gx)		
2. (x)(Fx ⊃ Gx) ⊃ (x)(Fx ⊃ ~Ex)		
3. (x)(Gx ⊃ Fx) ⊃ (x)(Gx ⊃ Px)		
4. (∃x)Fx	/∴	(∃x)(~Ex · Px)
5. Fa	4	EI

6. Fy ≡ Gy	1	UI
7. (Fy ⊃ Gy) · (Gy ⊃ Fy)	6	MEA
8. Fy ⊃ Gy	7	Simp
9. Gy ⊃ Fy	7	Simp
10. (x)(Fx ⊃ Gx)	8	UG
11. (x)(Gx ⊃ Fx)	9	UG
12. (x)(Fx ⊃ ~Ex)	2,10	MP
13. (x)(Gx ⊃ Px)	3,11	MP
14. Fa ⊃ ~Ea	12	UI
15. Ga ⊃ Pa	13	UI
16. ~Ea	14,5	MP
17. Fa ⊃ Ga	10	UI
18. Fa ⊃ Pa	17,15	HS
19. Pa	18,5	MP
20. ~Ea · Pa	16,19	Conj
21. (∃x)(~Ex · Px)	20	EG

Premises two and three never need to be instantiated.

99.
1. (∃x)(Mx · Tx)
2. (x)[Mx ⊃ (Hx · Wx)]
3. (x){[Sx · (Tx · Mx)] ⊃ Cx}
4. (x)(Cx ⊃ Lx)
5. (x)(Dx ⊃ Mx)
6. (x)[(Dx · Ax) ⊃ ~Sx]
7. (∃x)(Dx · ~Ax)   /∴ (x){[(Dx · ~Hx) · ~Ax] ⊃ Lx}

8. My ⊃ (Hy · Wy)	2	UI
9. Dy ⊃ My	5	UI
10. (Dy · ~Hy) · ~Ay		
11. Dy · ~H	10	Simp
12. Dy	11	Simp
13. ~Hy	11	Simp
14. My	9,12	MP
15. Hy · Wy	8,14	MP
16. Hy	15	Simp
17. Hy ∨ Ly	16	Add

18. Ly	17,13	DS
19. [Dy · (~Hy · ~Ay)] ⊃ Ly	10-18	CP
20. (x){[Dx · (~Hx · ~Ax)] ⊃ Lx}	19	UG

Premises 1, 3, 4, 6 and 7 are superfluous; and the antecedent of the conclusion contradicts premises 2 and 5. The argument is clearly unsound. It may also be invalid, if the apparent equivocation over the term 'hairless' is real. (Are "hairless" dogs, in fact hairless?)

100. 1. (x)(Tx ≡ Mx)		
2. (x)(Bx ⊃ ~Mx)		
3. (x)(Ex ⊃ Tx)		
4. (x)(Bx ⊃ ~Ex) ⊃ Rp	/∴	~Rp ⊃ (x)Tx
5. Ty ≡ My	1	UI
6. By ⊃ ~My	2	UI
7. Ey ⊃ Ty	3	UI
8. (Ty ⊃ My) · (My ⊃ Ty)	5	MEA
9. Ty ⊃ My	8	Simp
10. Ey ⊃ My	7,9	HS
11. ~My ⊃ ~Ey	10	Transp
12. By ⊃ ~Ey	6,11	HS
13. (x)(Bx ⊃ ~Ex)	12	UG
14. Rp	4,13	MP
15. Rp ∨ (x)Tx	14	Add
16. ~Rp ⊃ (x)Tx	15	MI

Made in the USA
Monee, IL
22 August 2021